THE PEOPLE AND THE BOOK

CASCADE COMPANIONS

The Christian theological tradition provides an embarrassment of riches: from Scripture to modern scholarship, we are blessed with a vast and complex theological inheritance. And yet this feast of traditional riches is too frequently inaccessible to the general reader.

The Cascade Companions series addresses the challenge by publishing books that combine academic rigor with broad appeal and readability. They aim to introduce nonspecialist readers to that vital storehouse of authors, documents, themes, histories, arguments, and movements that comprise this heritage with brief yet compelling volumes.

SOME OTHER TITLES IN THIS SERIES:

Cascade Companion to Evil by Charles Taliaferro
Reading Paul by Michael Gorman
The Rule of Faith by Everett Ferguson
The Second-Century Apologists by Alvyn Pettersen
Origen by Ronald E. Heine
Athanasius of Alexandria by Lois Farag
Basil of Caesarea by Andrew Radde-Gallwitz
Reading Augustine by Jason Byassee
A Guide to St. Symeon the New Theologian by Hannah Hunt
Thomas à Kempis by Greg Peters
Lutheran Theology by Paul R. Hinlicky
John Calvin by Donald K. McKim
Heinrich Bullinger by Donald K. McKim and Jim West
Jacob Arminius by Rustin E. Brian
Richard Hooker by W. Bradford Littlejohn
John Wesley by Henry H. Knight III
A Companion to Mercersburg Theology by William B. Evans
Reading Kierkegaard I by Paul Martens
Reading Bonhoeffer by John W. Matthews
Rudolph Bultmann by David W. Congdon
Jacques Ellul by Jacob E. Van Vleet and Jacob M. Rollinson
Understanding Pannenberg by Anthony C. Thiselton

THE PEOPLE AND THE BOOK

*Negotiating Religious Change in
Reformation England and Beyond*

CAROLINE
LITZENBERGER

 CASCADE *Books* • Eugene, Oregon

THE PEOPLE AND THE BOOK
Negotiating Religious Change in Reformation England and Beyond

Cascade Companions

Cascade Books
An Imprint of Wipf and Stock Publishers
199 W. 8th Ave., Suite 3
Eugene, OR 97401

www.wipfandstock.com

PAPERBACK ISBN: 978-1-6667-5108-6
HARDCOVER ISBN: 978-1-6667-5109-3
EBOOK ISBN: 978-1-6667-5110-9

Cataloguing-in-Publication data:

Names: Litzenberger, C. J. [author].

Title: The people and the book : negotiating religious change in Reformation England and beyond / Caroline Litzenberger.

Description: Eugene, OR: Cascade Books, 2022 | Series: Cascade Companions | Includes bibliographical references and index.

Identifiers: ISBN 978-1-6667-5108-6 (paperback) | ISBN 978-1-6667-5109-3 (hardcover) | ISBN 978-1-6667-5110-9 (ebook)

Subjects: LCSH: Reformation—England | England—Church history—16th century | England—Religious life and customs | Anglican Communion

Classification: BR375 L58 2022 (paperback) | BR375 (ebook)

10/20/22

CONTENTS

Acknowledgments • vii

Abbreviations • ix

Conventions • xi

Introduction • xiii

1   Prelude to Reform (1300–1520) • 1

2   Religious Change Challenges England (1520–46) • 16

3   England becomes Officially Protestant (1547–53) • 39

4   Marian Catholicism Reigns Supreme (1553–58) • 61

5   Elizabethan Religion, in All Its Diversity (1558–1603) • 81

6   The Story Continues (1603–Present) • 105

Conclusion • 138

Bibliography • 143

Index • 149

ACKNOWLEDGMENTS

FIRST AND BEFORE ALL else, I want to thank the people of St. Michael & All Angels in Portland, Oregon, my parish for much of the past fifty years, for showing me the importance of lay people in the life of the Church. I would also like to thank the people in various congregations and my fellow seminarians for their questions about parishioners' reactions to the many changes in religious policy during the English Reformation. That experience and these questions prompted me to write this book.

More particularly, I would like to thank the people who contributed directly to the content of this book: to the late Professor Patrick Collinson, my PhD supervisor at Cambridge University, since this work is based primarily, though by no means exclusively, on my PhD research; to the staffs of the Cambridge University Library, the Gloucester City Library, the Gloucestershire Record Office, the Wiltshire Record Office, the Borthwick Institute, the Cheshire Record Office, and the Essex Record Office; to the Rev. John Scannell and Professor Eric Josef Carlson, who both read and commented on the manuscript which became this book; to Mary Bowlby, who served as my first editor and source of encouragement; and to Janet Plog, who's unflagging support and patience all through the process of writing this book kept me going. Everyone who read or edited the manuscript shared with me the errors and awkward phrases they found; however, any remaining errors are mine and mine alone. My gratitude to each person who helped in this endeavor knows no bounds. I have been truly blessed.

ABBREVIATIONS

GRO   Gloucestershire Record Office

HWRO   Hereford and Worcestershire Record Office

L&P   Letters and Papers, Foreign and Domestic, of the Reign of Henry VIII

PRO   Public Records Office

VAI   Visitation Articles and Injunctions. Edited by Walter Howard Frere and William Paul McClure Kennedy.

CONVENTIONS

Two important terms have been standardized for ease of understanding by readers. The terms Catholic and Catholicism have been used for the traditional religion, the Church of Rome. The terms Protestant and Protestantism have been used for all sixteenth-century Evangelicals and others involved in the new religion which originated with Martin Luther, Ulrich Zwingli, and their followers in the German States and Switzerland.

INTRODUCTION

In the summer of 1551, the leaders of St. Michael's Parish in
Gloucester paid two laborers to remove the dirt from beneath
the altar and choir pews, so that the floor in the front portion
of the church would be level with the area where the worshipers sat for worship services. Then two years later, those
same leaders paid to have the dirt brought back, so that the
altar and choir pews could once again be elevated above the
level of the worshipers' pews. The process of removing the
dirt occurred again five years later when Elizabeth acceded
to the throne. So why were those men digging the dirt out in
St. Michael's parish in the autumn of 1551, putting it back just
two years later, and removing it again in 1559?[1]

---

1. GRO, St. Michael's Churchwardens Accounts, P154/14 CW 1/5.

RELIGIOUS CHANGE—IN THE FORM of the Reformation—did indeed come to England in the sixteenth century, with swings back and forth between traditional and new beliefs and practices, between various forms of Protestantism and Catholicism depending on the faith of the monarch. And yes, some of these changes did indeed result in the activity described above. All these changes raise some interesting questions:

- Where did the Church of England come from?

- How does the Reformation in England relate to the other Protestant Reformations (those in various European countries on the continent)?

- What was the role of the laity in English religious change? How did they respond to all the changes in religious policy?

- Why do the Church of England and other Anglican Churches look the way they do?

These questions will be addressed in this and subsequent chapters of this book.

EFFECTING RELIGIOUS CHANGE: AN OVERVIEW OF THE ENGLISH REFORMATION

From 1530 to 1603, as the monarch and bishops issued set after set of religious policies, they expected parishes and parishioners to adapt to each change, a challenge for all and an unrealistic expectation. England was far too complex a society. Further, the Church is the Body of Christ made up of countless living, breathing human beings who are all followers of Christ Jesus, each uniquely created in God's image. Each brings their God-given

gifts, their life experiences, and their personal percep-
tions to their faith, leading to much diversity within the
whole Body of Christ as to what each person believes.
They don't necessarily hear official religious policy the
same as their neighbors. This was especially true in
England in the sixteenth century, given its leaders' ap-
proaches to bringing Protestantism to the realm or restoring Catholicism.

The English Reformation, the series of religious
changes introduced during the sixteenth century in England, was a momentous development in the lives of the
people and in the realm. These changes opened new possibilities for parishes, clergy, and people across the realm
in that time and ever since. As we will see, these changes
and the resulting responses would eventually influence the
nature of Anglican and Episcopal churches today.

Early on, the challenge seems to have been to figure
out how to accommodate each new set of changes introduced by the Crown. However, as new changes followed
those previously introduced, and as some contradicted
those that had come before, many people began to examine their faith anew, paying less and less attention to
official religious policy and the religion of the monarch
as arbiters of "right religion." Rather, these became guide-
lines with which to affiliate or from which to differenti-
ate, as people shaped their own religious identities. The
result was a religion known for diversity within the unity
provided by the English Church through its policies and
Prayer Books. And while these processes of ongoing religious change and identity-formation may have gained
energy in the sixteenth century, they did not end with
Elizabeth I's death. Rather, they have continued to influence Anglicanism around the world and The Episcopal
Church in particular in the years since.

The draw of Protestantism was significant in England, as well as across the Channel in the German States, The Netherlands, Switzerland, and France during the sixteenth century, and this was a religious movement, even though it was facilitated to some extent (perhaps inadvertently) by Henry VIII's perceived need for a male heir. None the less, many, maybe most, people were reluctant to give up their old familiar religion. So, acceptance of the new religion was mixed and often slow or at least contested.

Ultimately, several factors contributed to the process of creating English Protestantism between the 1520s and about 1600. Many people from differing spheres provided impetus for the changes, including students at Oxford and Cambridge gathering in the 1520s to discuss Lutheran writings smuggled into England from the continent, and powerful Protestant preachers who shared Lutheran ideas during the later 1530s, especially in Gloucestershire and Worcestershire. These promoters of Protestantism also included merchants and seamen who had travelled to the continent, came home, and shared their experiences of Lutheran worship and teachings with their neighbors. And they included the chaplains and silkwomen in Ann Boleyn's court, as well.[2]

As archbishop from 1533 to 1555, Thomas Cranmer (with other religious leaders), introduced Protestantism gradually during Henry VIII's reign and then more aggressively while Edward VI was king. Then in the fall of 1553, Queen Mary I abruptly and decisively restored Catholicism to England and punished Protestants who refused to return to the old, traditional religion. And finally, in terms of sixteenth-century religious change, there was Queen Elizabeth

2. Silkwomen were elite women married to men who were both wool merchants and civic leaders. They wove ribbons from silk thread that were then used to decorate both men's and women's clothing in sixteenth-century England.

I, who sought to return England to Protestantism broadly construed. Each of these actions will be explored more fully in the following chapters of this book. However, a key factor in the overall process of changing peoples' religion will be addressed here.

As each change in religious policy was introduced, the people, whoever they were and wherever they were, had the opportunity to reshape their particular religious identities. It is probably true that most did not intentionally enter into such a process, opting instead to go along quietly with each official change (or not). Yet, many did purposefully engage in religious identity-formation, a process that was both internal and external (private and public). Scholars tell us that we develop our identities through a combination of differentiation and affiliation: separating ourselves from those with different beliefs; aligning ourselves with those who have similar beliefs. However, our identity-formation also involves our understanding of these identities: how we perceive them as we ponder them internally; and how our actions are outward expressions of these same identities.

This is an interactive process. As our understanding of our religious beliefs grows, so does our public expression of these beliefs, and it doesn't just happen once. It happens repeatedly, as we perceive the public expression of our religious identity and then go back and modify our internal understanding of it. During the sixteenth century, these processes took different forms at different times and led to varying conclusions. Additionally, similar processes of identity-formation were used by some parishes and communities to determine their corporate responses to changing official religious policies. The result was an English form of Protestantism that was marked not by uniformity but by *diversity within unity*.[3]

3. Litzenberger, "Will-making in Identity Formation"; Litzenberger,

LOCAL CHANGE IN ENGLAND: INTRODUCING PARISHES INVOLVED IN THE REFORMATION

This diverse yet unified Church was also a dynamic presence in each community where it was located, and that public presence changed over time. This book tells the story of the English Church during the period of the English Reformation, generally identified as between the 1520s (when continental reformers' ideas reached England) and 1603 (when Queen Elizabeth I died). With the backdrop of official policy determined by the monarch and the religious hierarchy, this book will focus on the people in the parishes, both clergy and laity, and the impact of official policy in those parishes. Thus, we began this introduction with a brief glimpse at the effect these changes had on one parish church. Moving forward, this story will focus on the effect of changes in religious policy on several parishes, as well as on changes in their worship spaces. It will also explore the particular beliefs of parishioners as expressed in their wills and actions.

A few parishes will receive special attention. These include Hadleigh in Suffolk, the various parishes in Shrewsbury (taken as a group), and Cirencester, Tewkesbury, and St. Michael's, Gloucester—all in Gloucestershire. Generally, parish leadership was either in the hands of the civic leaders, mainly merchants, or in those of the landed gentry, those wealthy landholders who ranked above the leaders of

---

"Community, Faith and Identity." In 2009, Peter Marshall published an article titled, "(Re)defining the English Reformation," in which he asserted that religious identity-formation led to the diversity that has marked English Protestantism from the time of the English Reformation to this day. More recently, he published a book on the English Reformation (*Heretics and Believers*), in which he discusses both religious identity and the consequential nature of the English Reformation. Working independently, we each have reached a similar conclusion.

the town and below the nobility. Among the churches that will receive attention here, civic leaders dominated. The exception is the churches in Shrewsbury, where the gentry held sway. As will be revealed, this distinction was not necessarily a predictor of acceptance of religious change. The reality was more complex than that. Of the featured parishes, St. Michael's, Gloucester was the most accepting of change, striving to comply with each new set of religious policies as promptly as possible, whether Protestant or Catholic. Meanwhile, Hadleigh was the most conflicted, despite having close ties to the archbishop of Canterbury and a powerful, well-connected rector in Rowland Taylor. The churches of Shrewsbury, influenced as they were by the local gentry, moved more definitively toward Protestantism than did the others. Cirencester and Tewkesbury lagged behind the others in embracing the new beliefs and worship practices, for the most part not initiating the process of change until the 1570s.

SIXTEENTH-CENTURY ENGLISH WILLS: A VIEW INTO THE BELIEFS OF THE LAITY

Sixteenth-century wills are a rich source of information about the faith of ordinary people, even though most were illiterate and had to rely on scribes to prepare their wills. During this period, wills typically included three sections: the bequest of the soul, the bequest of the body, and the bequest of the testator's worldly goods. In exploring the faith of the testator, the bequest of the soul, often called the will preamble, was most useful. People used will preambles as a way of defining their faith—actually, declaring their religious identity—publicly in the face of official policy, even though they could neither read nor write and so engaged a scribe to write their wills or at least write down what the testator dictated. It was one of the few ways women could speak (at least semi-publicly) of their beliefs. Some men chose this means as well. The choices of will preambles (or soul bequests) during Edward's reign show this quite clearly for both women and men. These preambles can be divided into three categories, based on their textual content: traditional, ambiguous, and Protestant. Will scribes were either known for one or another of these categories, or they offered testators a choice among a range of preambles across all categories to fit with the religion of the testator, whatever it might have been. A few testators—mainly Protestants, but also including some Catholics—dictated their own original preambles, typically to ensure that the words accurately reflected their personal beliefs (sometimes in great detail) about salvation. In any case, despite the involvement of scribes, testators could control the content of their wills, including the preambles. While some testators may have deferred to their scribe, who typically then picked an ambiguous preamble, a substantial proportion of people made the choice themselves.

The other factor in deciding about the content of one's will preamble was the risk of offending those in authority by violating religious policy. Interestingly, there does seem to have been a fear among the people that they could be punished when their wills were read, typically after death. However, there is little evidence of such punishment coming to fruition. Two exceptions are two men who died in the early 1530s leaving very different wills. In one case, the will preamble was markedly protestant, while the other was quite traditional. The Protestant testator was a member of the landed gentry in Gloucestershire, William Tracy; the other, who included a traditional preamble, was Thomas Brown, a grocer in Bristol. However, the one feature they had in common was that both testators failed to bequeath any money for invocations of the saints or for elaborate burials and commemorations. Both wills were initially refused probate. Eventually, Tracy's body was exhumed and burned, while Brown's will was ultimately granted probate. So, withholding money from the Church could imperil the disposition of the will or body of a testator. However, despite some peoples' fears, testators were not typically punished for the beliefs expressed in their wills, even though the fear of such retribution continued throughout most of the century.[4]

CHAPTER ORGANIZATION OF THIS BOOK

The chapters that follow, will respond to the questions raised at the beginning of this introduction by examining the successive waves of religious change initiated by each monarch.

The chapters will be organized chronologically, and each will be followed by a brief Study Guide:

- Prelude to reform (1300s–1520)

- Religious change challenges England (1520–46)

- England becomes Officially Protestant (1547–53)

- Marian Catholicism reigns supreme (1553–58)

- Elizabethan Protestantism, in all its diversity, becomes the norm (1559–1603)

- The story continues (1603–present)

- Conclusion

4. Craig and Litzenberger, "Wills as Religious Propaganda," 430.

1

PRELUDE TO REFORM

(1300–1520)

IN THE CENTURIES BEFORE the Reformation introduced Protestantism to England and the rest of Europe, the Christian Church went through multiple upheavals and renewals. Most of these occurred within monastic communities but ultimately affected the whole Church from the pope on down. However, while each of these corrected past errors, none led to the creation of a new kind of Christianity with new beliefs and new pious practices, as did the Reformation of the sixteenth century. Three important developments, all of which came between about 1300 and 1500, were so life-changing that they created an overwhelming longing for certainty among the people that they would indeed be saved—that they would move from this life to eternal life, wrapped in God's ever-loving arms. These developments were: chaos in the papacy leading to there being three popes in 1409; the coming of famine and the Black Death to the people of Europe; and new ideas arising from scholarship informed by Renaissance humanism.[1] Each of these ultimately called into question people's confidence in the medieval Church. Additionally, they tried the patience of some, leading to the creation of religious movements labeled as heresies in some places. All of these developments contribute in some way to our understanding of the origins of the Church of England.

PAPAL CHAOS AND THE BLACK DEATH

Several things did indeed happen in the fourteen century that shook people's confidence in the Church, and they all continued on into the fifteenth century. The first was the Great Schism, also known as the Avignon captivity of the papacy (by the French king, initially Philip the Fair). It began in 1327 and eventually led to a time when there were multiple popes, each asserting his authority over all of western Christendom. No one was sure who was in charge. No one was sure whom they could trust as they began to deal with the second challenge: the onset of a massive famine from 1315 to 1317 (with famines following every few years afterwards), and the Black Death, which reached England near the end of 1348. This combination of a devastating famine with a dreaded plague seemed to come out of nowhere. It attacked people of all levels of society, and most

---

1. Renaissance humanism, also referred to as "The New Learning," is not to be confused with secular humanism. Renaissance humanism was an intellectual movement grounded in the study of ancient Greek and Roman texts in their original languages and the methods used to analyze those texts. It dates from the work of Petrarch in fourteenth-century Italy and was used throughout much of Europe during the fifteenth and sixteenth centuries.

who contracted it died. Many towns lost as much as one third of their population.

The crux of the matter was that people thought both the famine and the plague were acts of God. What else could they be? There was at the time no knowledge of science to explain either the origins or the rapid spread of either, but especially of this deadly disease. So, they surmised, God must be very angry with them! Mainly people in towns died, but so did some elite people who had isolated themselves in their manors, or so they thought. The elite still needed their food and fine wines, and the bottles of wine were sometimes packed in rat-infested straw. (Of course, they had no idea that fleas on rats spread the plague.)

In response, most of society turned to the clergy for guidance and relief. But then many clergy died and weren't replaced. So, to whom should the people turn next? In those cases, in the English Diocese of Salisbury, the bishop authorized the laity to turn to a well-educated lay man or woman! For the clergy who did survive, which pope should they trust to lead them out of this terrifying situation, given that the Great Schism often resulted in multiple popes with different allegiances? In particular, the English did not trust the pope residing in Avignon and under the authority of the French king. This was a daunting and scary situation. The peoples's lives hung in the balance, but even more than that, their souls were at risk. When they died—and given that death from the plague seemed nearly inevitable, it was "when," not "if"—would their souls live on with God in heaven? Regrettably, no matter what popes, bishops, and priests said or did, the Black Death raged on. The people could not count on the Church of Rome for answers to their questions.

Throughout this period, people focused more and more on their own mortality, and the Church's theology of salvation took on overwhelming importance. The religious leaders appeared to be unable to appease God or otherwise stem the tide of death, and fear overwhelmed most of the people of Europe. The disease did disappear after a few years, but it returned with a vengeance roughly every twenty years for about the next two hundred years. Many saw this phenomenon as proof that the Church was fatally flawed, and of course, the multiplicity of popes did not help. What was really wrong? What were the people doing wrong? Why was the Church saying the same old things? They weren't helping! God still seemed to be angry. Death still reigned supreme.

THE RENAISSANCE

Meanwhile, the Renaissance flourished in Italy. It first manifested itself in painting, sculpture, and architecture, then in Renaissance humanism, also known as the "New Learning." This was a new approach to scholarship and research, and it included a methodology for determining the dates of key documents, based on the form of Latin or Greek found there. This method of analysis was known as philology. The older the source the more reliable it was thought to be. Initially, this humanism focused on the writings of ancient Rome (in their original Latin), and then on those of ancient Greece (in the original Greek). Then, as more and more scholars from northern Europe flocked to Italian cities to learn from Renaissance scholars, the focus shifted to the Scriptures in their earliest form (in their original Greek or Hebrew), and to the fifth- and sixth-century writings of the early "Church fathers," also known as the "doctors" of the Church: Saints Anselm, Jerome, and Augustine, and Pope Gregory the Great. This scholarship revealed countless ways the policies, characteristics, and pious practices of the late-medieval institutional Church had moved away from the teachings of these earlier, more trusted documents and authorities. The Church seemed to have lost its way. These findings called into question the authority of the medieval church—the soundness of its doctrine and practices—at a time when it was struggling to respond effectively to the Black Death.

This New Learning, however, did more than highlight what was wrong with the medieval Church. It also offered a way forward: a vision of a renewal, based both on the values and writings of those "Church doctors," and on the even earlier versions of the Scriptures. The Bible then authorized by the Catholic Church contained countless errors, mainly resulting from inaccurate copying of earlier texts (multiple generations of earlier texts). This vision of a renewed, more authentic Church, in turn, offered hope to those languishing under the recurring threat of the Black Death and the seeming ineffectiveness of the Church of Rome. In the sixteenth century, this vision would inform religious leaders all over Europe, including those who moved outside the authority of the traditional Church to create new sets of beliefs, new theologies, new pieties, new worship practices, and ultimately new denominations, like Martin Luther in the German states, and Ulrich Zwingli and John Calvin in Switzerland. These three leaders of reform will be discussed more fully in the following chapters.

THE FLOURISHING OF THE "OLD RELIGION"

Despite the challenges to the Catholic Church in the medieval period, throughout the fifteenth and much of the sixteenth centuries, western Christianity based in Rome continued to flourish. The rhythm of the recurring struggles against the Black Death had become a part of the "new normal." Having survived the "bad old fourteenth century," when there were multiple popes and the Black Death raged, people settled into the new but increasingly familiar rhythm of life. For the most part, it was still those at the bottom of the social structure that died of the plague. The elite, for the most part, were spared. Life went on. Those with sufficient wealth rebuilt their parish churches from the ground up, while those with fewer resources still found ways to refurbish theirs. On any given day, people, whether merchants or people who worked the land, whether women or men, flocked to their parish churches to see the elevation of the Host at the high point of the Mass, when they heard the *sanctus* bell ring. This bell was affixed to the roof of the church with a rope dangling down inside, alongside the acolyte at the high altar. He would ring it at the appropriate time. The laity also prayed for their deceased forebears, prayed their rosaries, and bequeathed the customary sum to the high altar of their parish churches at the time of their deaths.

The familiar, the "old religion," still held a powerful draw. Lay participation in traditional religious worship and practices fed the people spiritually. However, developments in late-medieval Catholic piety and the discoveries of Renaissance humanism gave hope to those who had been frustrated by the Great Schism and by the ineffectiveness of the Church of Rome in the face of the terrifying menace of the Black Death. This led some to pour money into refurbishing their churches. Those who could afford it—mainly wealthy wool merchants—razed the naves and porches of their churches and rebuilt them in the latest, grandest style, as happened in Lavenham in Suffolk and Chipping Camden in Gloucestershire. Those with more limited funds focused on redecorating their interiors. In Cirencester, Gloucestershire the merchants collaborated on repainting their interior and even added a new chantry chapel. They also decorated the ceiling of the nave with their crests.

Meanwhile, St. Mary's, Fairford in Gloucestershire and St. Michael's in York added gorgeous stained-glass windows fashioned by the artisans King Henry VI had brought over from the continent to install new windows in King's College Chapel in Cambridge, a project that was not completed, thanks to the War of the Roses.

LATE-MEDIEVAL CHALLENGES TO THE "OLD RELIGION"

Both the developments in late-medieval piety, and the discoveries of Renaissance humanism offered possibilities of a new way forward for the Catholic Church and its many faithful followers. The late-medieval movement that opened the door to lay piety very similar to that of their monastic neighbors was called *devotio moderna* (or "modern devotion"). It was created by Gerhard Groote of The Netherlands. His followers founded a religious organization known as The Brethren of the Common Life which embraced education as their primary ministry. Both Martin Luther of Germany and the great Renaissance scholar Desiderius Erasmus of The Netherlands were students of this order. And ultimately, young women as well as young men would benefit from this ministry.

Meanwhile, both the discoveries and the methodologies of Renaissance Humanism would also affect religious change going forward. This movement insisted on returning to early sources to find the purest, most accurate form of knowledge, language, beliefs, and institutions, and as the Renaissance spread across northern Europe, the focus of scholars shifted from Greco-Roman sources to the Scriptures. This led Christian humanists (as these scholars are known) to call into question the validity and efficacy of traditional

Christian practices and beliefs. Desiderius Erasmus, who lived from c. 1469 to 1536, was a leader in this movement.

Erasmus, as he was known, became so famous for his learning and literary skills that he dominated the world of letters in Europe. He travelled around Europe through most of his adult life, spending two substantial periods in England, where he influenced the spread of humanist learning. He wrote his satirical book *In Praise of Folly* while a guest in the home of Sir Thomas More and taught for a time at Cambridge while living in Queen's College there. Through his writings and his travels, he hoped to restore the unity of European Christendom, which he saw as having been divided by the early reformers, including Luther in Germany and Zwingli in Switzerland. His humanism emphasized the inwardness of religion, the need for virtuous living, and moral social relationships. He used ancient wisdom to try to redress contemporary values. He applied his knowledge of Latin and Greek to understand the Bible better, approaching each gospel and each epistle as an entity to be understood as a unit. He applied this approach to reading the Bible more and more thoroughly, in combination with the application of humanist philological techniques to search texts for the correct meaning of words (the foundation of modern biblical criticism and thus influencing modern theology and the sermons proclaimed every Sunday). Erasmus believed that human beings had sufficient free will to decide whether to accept or reject God's offer of salvation, a point on which he differed sharply from Luther. He also believed that without faith it was not possible to please God, and that the sacraments and other good works would then be of no avail as aids to an individual's salvation.

It was not only new forms of piety and scholarship that presented challenges to the Catholic Church. There were also movements characterized by beliefs that fundamentally challenged the accepted faith. Key among these was the one religious movement that originated in England: Lollardy. The founder of this movement was The Rev. John Wycliffe, a scholar at Oxford, who died in 1384 and who had developed a set of rather radical ideas. He

- questioned the rightfulness of ecclesiastical possession of property.

- challenged the doctrine of papal supremacy over the Church, a doctrine based on the alleged designation of Peter as the head of the Church. ("On this rock I will found my Church.") In connection with this, he:

- opposed the paying of "Peter's pence," a papal tax typically collected through the parishes on Pentecost.

- criticized the papal curia, monks, and friars for their vices.

Additionally, he:

- attacked the special powers and privileges of the clergy;

- argued that scripture alone declared the will of God. No theologian or other member of the clergy, not even the pope, should tell people what they should believe;

- challenged the doctrine of transubstantiation, which had originated during the Fourth Lateran Council of 1215 (describing how Jesus Christ was present in the Eucharist);

- claimed that the only true Church was comprised only of the predestined (those already chosen by God to be saved, and therefore in a state of sanctified grace), and that only the elect could rule the elect;

- supported divesting popes and bishops of their property and their positions, and asserted they had no right to rule;
- asserted that the chief responsibility for ecclesiastical reform rested with the prince (king), and the prince determined how much authority the pope would be allowed to exercise.

He also began a translation of the Bible in 1382 but died two years later without finishing it.

Wycliffe's followers were known as Lollards. Initially, they included key and important people in the English court, but when he challenged transubstantiation, they turned away from him. More generally, this movement tended to emerge in regions where it was difficult to enforce official policy. Lollards met in houses, often at night. Ideas were exchanged and information imparted. Bible texts were read or recited and learned by heart. That seems to be all that happened in these gatherings. There is no evidence of praying, sharing the sacraments, or any formal ceremonies of initiation or singing. Each group was supported locally, often by substantial local gentry. (The old idea that Lollards were all from the lower classes is not accurate, according to the most recent research; Lollardy appealed to the whole social spectrum, except maybe the poorest of the poor and the wealthiest nobles.)

Wycliffe was declared a heretic by the pope in 1377; however, he was not prosecuted as a heretic. He died of natural causes five years later. His followers were persecuted by the English Crown, but they continued to meet and share their scriptural texts, and there is some evidence that some groups were still functioning 120 years later, at the time of the English Reformation. Thus, this movement may well have contributed to the acceptance of Protestantism in sixteenth-century England.

Meanwhile, Wycliffe's teachings spread beyond England, thanks to Jan Hus of Bohemia, who travelled to Oxford to study with him. After Hus returned home, he became an eloquent preacher, espousing some of Wycliffe's ideas, although his theology was (as best we can tell) more conservative than Wycliffe's. In his view, the Church included only the predestined. He also questioned (but did not deny) transubstantiation. He won a large following among the common people, who were known as Hussites; however, he was seen as a threat by the Catholic Church. In 1415 he was summoned to appear at the Church's Council of Constance where the primary concern was reuniting western Christendom under a single pope. He was reluctant to show up but was promised safe travel. However, when he arrived, he was arrested and then burned at the stake as a heretic.

Nonetheless, the Hussites were not eliminated as a result of Hus's death. Not even a special crusade could accomplish that. Rather, the next Council after Constance, held at Basel from 1431 to 1449, reached a diplomatic settlement with the moderate wing of the Hussite movement, granting them communion in 1436. This movement represents one of the earliest successful revolts against the medieval religious establishment. It was also the first withdrawal of an entire territory (that is, Bohemia) from religious unity with Rome.

CONTINENTAL AND ENGLISH APPROACHES TO RELIGIOUS CHANGE

Meanwhile, many religious leaders were among those who looked forward to changes in beliefs and practices: more specifically, to the introduction of Protestantism (or "right religion," as it was known) in some form in their regions of influence. Protestantism was a logical outgrowth of the discoveries of Renaissance humanism, but also (interestingly) of *devotio moderna* (the evolving conventional medieval theology discussed earlier). The ideas and beliefs arising from such intellectual efforts led naturally to Protestantism. And this new religion offered hope to many, especially those who carried the burden or threat of the Black Death in their hearts. The Church of Rome had come up short when they longed for assurance of their salvation. It had similarly failed to blunt the effects of that dreaded disease. The very real threat of death hung over everyone. Protestantism offered a way forward that included certainty of salvation, based on faith in God's saving grace.

Protestantism was an attractive alternative to traditional religion in England, as well as on the continent across the English Channel. However, the focus and methods of bringing the people to this new religion would differ between England and the rest of Europe. In the early Church, worship had formed beliefs: *lex orandi . . . lex credendi* (the pattern/rule of prayer is the pattern/rule of belief). Worship arising from Jesus's teachings and actions was developed first. In particular, Holy Communion (the Eucharist), and the rite of Baptism were established as liturgical rites and sacraments during the first centuries after Christ. Next came the theology needed to explain the liturgy, which in turn influenced the liturgy. This dynamic interactive pattern of worship influencing theology and then theology influencing worship would continue, *ad infinitum*.

While this influence of worship and theology on each other holds true for all Christian denominations, the continental reformers differed from their counterparts in England as to the best way to effect change initially. On the continent, Martin Luther was quite clear in asserting that doctrine, which defined acceptable beliefs, should come first when changing the beliefs of worshippers. Revisions in liturgy would then follow and support the new doctrine. Zwingli, and later, Calvin in Switzerland proceeded in a similar manner. It was important to inculcate the people with "right beliefs" first, and then "right worship" would follow. Meanwhile in England, Thomas Cranmer and the other leaders involved in changing English religion believed the opposite. They thought that it was more effective to change worship first: to design worship to reflect "right beliefs." Then, as parishioners repeatedly followed the new liturgy, their beliefs would be shaped by that worship, rather than the other way around. The English Church would thus be defined as a *liturgical* church, while the churches that emerged during the Reformation on the continent would become *doctrinal* churches—churches defined by their "right beliefs."

This distinction would shape much of the experience of members of churches on both sides of the Channel. Additionally, focusing initially on worship in English churches would result in a broad range of beliefs across the kingdom—what some scholars have described as diversity within unity: diverse beliefs within the one Church in (and of) England. Referring to the modern Episcopal Church in the United States, The Rev. John Westerhoff (professor of theology and Christian nurture at Duke University and Christian educator) says,

> We understand Christianity as a way of life . . . , rather than a theory, in which religion and morality, theology and ethics are one. . . . Our primary identity is as a community of practice . . . , bound together by our liturgy rather than [our doctrine]. Orthodoxy for us is right worship and not right belief. Our life of prayer shapes our beliefs and behaviors.[2]

2. Westerhoff, *A People Called Episcopalians*, 3.

This description may refer to the modern Church, but it is also an accurate description of Cranmer's Church and of most Churches established by the Church of England in different countries over the years since the early 1550s, all known eventually as Anglican Churches. Grounded in worship, the beliefs of its members are indeed varied, but they come together at the altar to share Holy Communion, the Eucharist, with one another. They worship together. This identity may have frustrated many over the centuries, but it would endure.

RELIGIOUS CHANGE IN SIXTEENTH-CENTURY ENGLAND

Religious change became the watchword in sixteenth-century England, as each monarch's religious policy reflected their personal beliefs or those of the most powerful people around them. That is, the contours of the English Reformation were largely defined by the monarchs. This reality, in turn, probably caused truly faithful Christians who were also faithful subjects of the Crown to experience some form of "spiritual whiplash" as they sought to do what was "right" at each particular moment during the English Reformation.

Most religious leaders in England during the second half of the reign of Henry VIII, and especially during the reign of his son, Edward VI, espoused and promoted Protestant beliefs. However, in England between the reigns of Edward VI and Elizabeth I, Mary Tudor reigned for five years. She had been born a Catholic and would die as such. During her five years on the throne, she returned England to the Catholic fold, even though this policy may have brought concern to some leaders, especially to members of Parliament who had benefited financially from the previous anti-Catholic policies. However, for most parishioners,

Mary's reign brought sighs of relief and much joy. The introduction of Protestantism under Henry and Edward, whatever its manifestation, had left the people longing for the traditional rites and pious practices of earlier years—rites and practices that in their familiarity had fed their souls and comforted them in the midst of their trials and tribulations. Elizabeth's accession to the throne and her early religious policies may have initially brought confusion, but later her policies did define a form of Protestantism, and gradually a large proportion of the people came around.

BEYOND SIXTEENTH-CENTURY RELIGIOUS CHANGE

Elizabeth I's reign was long enough for the liturgy to become familiar. Then as England moved into and through the seventeenth century and beyond, the Church and the people would experience more change. Eventually, the resulting Church, both in England and around the world, would become the one we know today.

DISCUSSION QUESTIONS

1. Why did so many priests not trust the popes during the Great Schism?

2. Why do you think people panicked as the Black Death spread?

3. What did Renaissance humanism contribute to sixteenth-century religious change?

4. How would the Protestant Reformation have been different without contributions from Renaissance humanism?

2

RELIGIOUS CHANGE CHALLENGES ENGLAND

(1520–46)

Protestantism came to England during Henry VIII's reign. Across Europe the ground had been prepared for this new faith, thanks to the challenges of the papal schism, the Black Death, Renaissance humanism, and yes, even heresies like Lollardy and the Hussites. England, along with the rest of Europe, had been a part of western Christendom under the authority of the Catholic Church and the pope based in Rome. In England, five different versions of the Mass (Holy Communion) were used in different parts of the kingdom. However, the version used by most was the Sarum Rite, so named for its origin in the Diocese of Salisbury. In the reign of Edward VI, this rite would form the basis for the Holy Communion service in the new *Book of Common Prayer*; however, while Henry VIII was king, the several different versions of the Mass was still used, depending on the location of the parish church. Meanwhile, as more and more people and clergy were exposed to Lutheran Protestantism—whether in person or through Lutheran writings—religious policies began to shift, even while Henry was still king. The story of this period will contribute further to our understanding of the origins of the Church of England, to the relationship of the burgeoning English Reformation to other Protestant Reformations, and to the role of the laity in religious change in England. Additionally, it will touch on the origins of the Church of England in terms of its liturgy, including the connection between pre-Reformation worship and the first *Prayer Books*.

By the mid-1520s scholars in both Oxford and Cambridge were gathering in taverns to discuss theological books smuggled into England by merchants, scholars, and even the Queen's chaplains. Beginning nearly a decade earlier, Martin Luther in the German States and Ulrich Zwingli in Switzerland had both started introducing religious changes in their regions of Europe. Martin Luther and his followers, in particular, used the printing press to spread their ideas. Many of these books were printed in English by continental printers. Scholars and others in England welcomed these works, read them, and discussed them. Those talking about them included a number of future English Protestant religious leaders, including Thomas Cranmer.

However, it wasn't just scholars who were exposed to Protestantism in the 1520s. Seamen on ships that docked at German ports and merchants involved in trading with their German counterparts in German cities worshipped in Lutheran churches and returned to England to tell their friends and neighbors about their experiences. The told about parts of the worship being in the language of the people, rather than it all being in Latin, and about singing hymns in German, as well. Did they find it strange or wonderful? We don't know, but we do know that they shared their experiences with others once they returned to England.

THE RISE OF CONTINENTAL PROTESTANTISM

The story of the Protestant Reformation begins with Luther in Germany and Zwingli in Switzerland. These two reformers had different educational backgrounds and different goals, but much of their theology was identical. They both worked to bring what became known as Protestantism to their regions of influence. Luther was an Augustinian monk who had been influenced by the evolving medieval theology, while Zwingli was the product of Renaissance humanism, which had spread widely outside Italy. Both received support from city leaders, as did other reformers working with them, perhaps because (at least in the German States) it was a way to blunt the local power of the Spanish Holy Roman emperor, whom civic leaders resented. Both encouraged their followers to read the Bible. Luther translated it into German by 1524, the same year a French version was published. Zwingli merely benefited from the sudden availability of the Scriptures in the vernacular. His sermons were always based on Scripture, as were Luther's. These Scripture-focused sermons marked a departure from earlier themes of doctrine and saint's lives in most traditional sermons.

More particularly, these two men agreed on three key theological points:

- While the traditional Church taught that divine authority, God's authority, came through the Church hierarchy's interpretation of Scripture and tradition, Luther and Zwingli believed that Scripture itself was the only source of divine authority—*sola scriptura*. Therefore, ordinary people should have direct access to the Scriptures. Hence the need for translations into the vernacular.

- While the traditional Church taught that salvation came through good works, which were the fruits of faith (including donations, sacraments, prayers and intercessions, to name a few), both Luther and Zwingli declared that salvation came by faith alone—*sola fide*—faith in the redeeming power of Christ's resurrection. They believed that God had chosen those who would believe the gospel and be saved, hence they were known as "the elect."

- The traditional church declared that there were seven sacraments, but Luther and Zwingli pointed out that only two are found in Scripture, and therefore there are only two—baptism and Holy Communion—since Scripture is the sole source of divine authority.

On other beliefs they disagreed:

- Concerning sacraments:

    - Luther believed that sacraments were conduits of God's grace *in the present moment*.

    - Zwingli believed that they were signs and seals of God's grace *previously given*.

    - (The traditional Church taught that sacraments were a means of grace and that receiving these sacraments was a good work, which was the path to salvation.)

- Concerning the Eucharist:

  ◆ Luther believed Christ's body and blood were actually, physically present alongside the bread and wine, although he was indifferent as to the means by which this happens. (This is similar to the traditional Church's belief in transubstantiation, but in the case of the latter, the bread and wine are believed to be physically transformed into the body and blood of Christ through the words and actions of the priest in the Mass.)

  ◆ Zwingli believed that the Eucharist was a commemoration of the Last Supper: the institution of the Eucharist by Jesus shortly before he was arrested by the Romans.

- When contemplating images, whether statues, paintings, stained glass, or organ music

  ◆ Luther agreed with the traditional Church, that they were "poor people's books:" a way for the illiterate to learn "right beliefs."

  ◆ Zwingli saw them as dangerous, pernicious idols that could potentially lead the people to worship them, instead of worshipping God.

Luther's ideas and those of his followers would initially hold sway in England. Their books were the ones discussed in the taverns of Cambridge and Oxford, and it was Lutheran churches that merchants and seamen attended when they were in German cities. However, as Henry VIII's reign was drawing to a close, Zwingli's ideas, especially those concerning images, began to influence some clergy and lay people in some regions of England.

THE INFLUENCE OF LUTHERAN WRITINGS ON SCHOLARS IN CAMBRIDGE AND OXFORD

The ideas of the continental reformers—especially, at this point, those of Luther—caught the attention of both scholars and those involved in trade with German cities, as noted earlier. It is the scholars on whom we will focus next. This is one of the ways the Reformation in England was connected to those on the continent. These scholars included many future leaders of the Church of England, including at least two future archbishops of Canterbury: Thomas Cranmer (from 1533 to 1555), and Matthew Parker (from 1559 to 1575). Additionally, the great preacher and rector of Hadleigh parish, Rowland Taylor; the bishop of London under Edward VI, Nicholas Ridley; and the biblical scholar William Tyndale, participated in the discussions of these Lutheran books.

Tyndale, who studied at Oxford, became tutor to two boys in the Gloucestershire household of a member of the county elite in 1524, where he began translating the Bible into English, as well as teaching the boys. He would return to Oxford and eventually flee to the continent, where he would continue his translation of the Bible—a project that the king and his minions tried to suppress. Although Tyndale died before completing it, his Bible would be finished by another reformer and good friend of Tyndale's, John Rogers, alias Thomas Matthews, and be known as the *Matthews Bible*. It would be the first Bible in English to receive widespread, although unauthorized, distribution. Subsequently the *Great Bible* appeared; however, most of its Old Testament was translated from the (Latin) Vulgate Bible or other recent version and contained many errors. The *Great Bible* was the first Bible in English authorized for use in England, but in 1539 it was replaced by the much more accurate *Bishop's Bible*.

While Tyndale was in Gloucestershire, he met many local elites, including Sir William Tracy, who impressed him sufficiently with his theological knowledge that Tyndale made note of the fact. Later, when writing his remarkable will, Tracy would echo the beliefs espoused by both Luther and Zwingli (and indeed, Tyndale). He began his will, written in 1531 with the words,

> First and before all other thing, I commit me unto God, and to his mercy, trusting without any doubt or mistrust, that by his grace and the merits of Jesus Christ, and by the virtue of his passion and of his resurrection, I have and shall have remission of my sins and resurrection of body and soul, according as it is written Job xix. I believe that my redeemer lives, and that in the last day I shall rise out of the earth, and in my flesh shall see my Savior, this my hope is laid up in my bosom.

He continued:

> And as touching the wealth of my soul, the faith that I have taken and rehearsed is sufficient (as I suppose) without any other man's work or works. My ground and my belief is that there is but one God and one mediator between God and man, which is Jesus Christ. So that I do accept none in heaven nor in earth to be my mediator between me and God but only Jesus Christ, all other be but petitioners in receiving of grace, but none able to give influence of grace. And therefore will I bestow no part of my goods for that intent

> that any man should say or do to help my soul:
> for therein I trust only to the promise of God, he
> that believes and is baptized shall be saved, and
> he that believes not shall be damned, Mark the
> last chapter.[1]

His declaration of faith was woven throughout his entire will, including the clauses where he bequeathed his body and his worldly goods, and it quickly attracted significant attention. Before the end of the year in which it was written, multiple copies were in the hands of people across the realm. By 1535 it had been printed in a pamphlet with commentaries by Tyndale and fellow co-religionist John Frith. The first will known to have been influenced by Tracy's distinctive preamble appeared in 1537, prepared at the direction of William Shepherd of Mendlesham in Suffolk. Most of his first paragraph was a *verbatim* copy of Tracy's, with a parenthetical explanation added. What followed was also primarily lifted from Tracy's will.[2]

As with Tracy, William Shepherd's faith permeated his entire will. Many who embraced a form of Protestantism used portions of Tracy's will to declare publicly their religious identities. Wills inspired by Tracy's continued to appear at least into the 1640s.[3] These two examples contribute to our understanding of the role of the laity in the English Reformation. They used their wills to express their faith and to influence others.

Wills were but one way people expressed their Protestant faith. Some also proclaimed their faith in sermons and pamphlets. These included an East Anglian priest, Thomas Bilney, and a nephew of William Tracy, James Baynham. Baynham was a layman from Westbury-upon-Severn, the

1 *The Testament of Master Wylliam Tracie,* sigs Aiii-iii.

2. Craig and Litzenberger, "Wills as Religious Propaganda," 425–26.

3. Craig and Litzenberger, "Wills as Religious Propaganda," 428.

largest town in the Forest of Dean in Gloucestershire. Both were convicted of heresy and burned because of their beliefs. Bilney was burned in August 1531 in Norwich. Baynham was burned at Smithfield in London in April 1532.

THE KING'S "GREAT MATTER"

A myth still persists, asserting that the English Reformation was entirely the result of King Henry VIII's desire for a second wife and a male heir. And while that is a significant overstatement, it would probably be accurate to see those desires as smoothing the way for the Protestant advances in official religious policy in England in the early 1530s. By then Protestantism had already attracted the interest of laymen and clergy, as noted earlier, although Henry VIII would remain a Catholic until he died.

Henry's perceived need for a male heir was real, at least in his eyes. His father had gained the crown by battle, but Henry had been fortunate enough to ascend to the throne without incident at his father's death. However, Henry's only child in the 1520s was female, and no female had ever been crowned monarch of England. The daughter of Henry I had tried without success in the early twelfth century, although her son and Henry I's grandson would eventually attain the throne and reign as Henry II.

The situation in the 1520s thus presented Henry VIII with a daunting and worrisome challenge. His first attempt at a solution was to legitimize his illegitimate son, Henry Fitzroy; however, that young man died shortly afterwards in 1524. Next, he turned to the possibility that God was punishing him for having married the widow of his deceased brother, Arthur, in violation of the Levitical Code, even though he had received a papal dispensation before marrying her. Through his secretary, Cardinal Wolsey, and others, Henry attempted to mount diplomatic pressure and petitioned the pope for an annulment from his marriage to Catharine of Aragon. Unfortunately, his timing was terrible. At that time, the pope was being held captive by Catherine's nephew, King Charles V of Spain, the Holy Roman emperor. No annulment would be forthcoming.

As a result, under the leadership of Thomas Cromwell, the king's new secretary, England began moving away from its subservience to the Church in Rome and the papacy. Through a series of royal proclamations and parliamentary statutes, English subjects were prohibited from appealing English Church court decisions to Rome. Additionally, taxes previously paid to the pope were now paid to the Crown, and the king became the "supreme head" of the Church in England.

Perhaps more importantly in Henry's mind, he was able to take the steps he felt necessary to ensure the monarchy would remain in his family; the succession would be secured. Thomas Cranmer, the new archbishop of Canterbury issued a divorce decree, ending the king's first marriage and freeing him to marry Anne Boleyn. Cranmer then presided at the king's marriage to Anne.

THE OFFICIAL INTRODUCTION OF PROTESTANTISM IN ENGLAND IN THE 1530S

Following the arrival and discussion of continental Protestant writings, and the sharing of experiences of Protestant worship, some in England were ready to start making changes in official religious policy. The three people who played key roles in this effort were:

- Thomas Cromwell, the king's secretary, who had previously been a merchant and had probably been educated in Renaissance Italy and converted to Lutheranism before returning to England.

- Anne Boleyn, Henry VIII's second wife, who before she caught his eye had received a Renaissance education at the French court, and while there, had probably also been exposed to Lutheranism.

- Thomas Cranmer, who was named archbishop of Canterbury by Henry based on Anne's recommendation, and who had secretly converted to Lutheranism and married the niece of a prominent follower of Luther while serving as one of the king's ambassadors on the continent before becoming archbishop.

There is clear evidence of their collaboration in promoting reform, and specifically, in spreading Lutheran beliefs in the 1530s. Unfortunately, they did not all live to see the fruits of their labors. Anne Boleyn, having become queen as Henry's second wife and having given birth to Elizabeth, who would one day become Queen Elizabeth I, was falsely accused of treason against the king by powerful men opposed to Lutheranism. She was beheaded in 1536. Four years later, Thomas Cromwell would experience a similar fate at the hands of that same group. The only one to survive was Cranmer, who continued as archbishop of Canterbury and was responsible for the creation of the first two *Books of Common Prayer* of the Church of England, during the reign of Henry VIII's successor, Edward VI.

While she lived, Anne Boleyn influenced religious change in at least two ways: by patronage and book smuggling. She used her patronage to see that at least two priests were elevated to the episcopate or archiepiscopate. Latimer became bishop of Worcester and Cranmer became archbishop of Canterbury. She was also involved in bringing reformers' writings into England. She had her chaplains smuggle books into the realm and into her private chambers. Some she gave to the king to read. Others were placed where they could be read by her ladies in waiting and her silkwomen, including Joan Wilkinson, wife of a prominent London merchant who would later figure prominently in supporting those destined for martyrdom in Mary I's reign. After Queen Anne had been imprisoned, William Latimer, one of her chaplains, was caught with prohibited Protestant books when he re-entered England. He was arrested but was allowed to send those books to Joan Wilkinson, and she, in turn, later shared them with the radical Protestant bishop of Gloucester, John Hooper, who would serve in that capacity during the reign of Edward VI.[4]

Cromwell, Cranmer, and Queen Anne were all involved in introducing Lutheran Protestantism into official English religious policy in the 1530s. Changes in policy were made through the first half of the decade which effectively severed the relationship between the papacy and the English Church. Then three developments ratcheted up the intensity of reform in the second half of that decade: Hugh Latimer became bishop of Worcester in 1535; the First Act for the Dissolution of the Monasteries was approved by Parliament in 1536; and sets of Royal Proclamations pertaining to religion were promulgated in 1536 and 1538.

Soon after Hugh Latimer was named bishop of Worcester (which included both Worcestershire and Gloucestershire), he developed a team of preachers who believed as he did and effectively spread these Protestant beliefs to all the corners of his diocese. One such corner was the dark and forbidding Royal Forest of Dean, covered with thick woods, populated mainly by illiterate free miners, and

4. *L&P*, vol. X, no. 827; Dowling, "Anne Boleyn and Reform," 33.

characterized by limited access, giving it a sense of isolation and possibly freedom from authority.[5]

There, Latimer's preachers found an audience ready to embrace the new religious teachings and create new religious identities. In one case, a man who had apparently heard one of these preachers declared that he would rather "confess himself to a tree than to a priest," thus refuting private confession.[6] On another occasion, a group gathered at a mill to discuss various theological issues. One declared that the bread and wine of the Eucharist could not be the actual body and blood of Christ, because "Christ had taken his own body with him up to heaven and had not left it behind."[7] A similar, if less explicit, rejection of the traditional eucharistic belief of the real presence was made at about the same time at a gathering of like-minded people at a house in another part of the Forest. Ordinary people were discussing theology, thanks to effective and energetic preaching under the direction of Bishop Latimer. Additionally, they were acting on some of these new theological ideas, including engaging in lay Bible reading, or at least hearing the Bible read by one of the few literate members of their group.[8]

However, having unleashed such negative energy against the traditional Church, the preachers could not necessarily control their hearers. One night, as people deep within the Forest of Dean approached their church for the evening service, they saw two men standing outside the door to the church next to the basin of holy water. One said to the other, "Drop your drawers." He then said, "Remember your baptism," the words Latimer had instructed all his priests to use when sprinkling parishioners with

5. Wabuda, "The Provision of Preaching," 109–12.

6. HWRO, 802 BA 2764, 109–10.

7. HWRO, 802 BA 2764, 115.

8. Brigden, *London and the Reformation*, 281–82.

holy water. In this case, though, it was not a priest but a lay person who did the sprinkling, and rather than sprinkling the holy water on the other man's head, he sprinkled it on his rear. This was a clear, if shocking, demonstration that he didn't believe the water he was sprinkling held any particular power or significance, and that traditional practice was a manifestation of superstition. The bishop and his preachers may still have believed in the special place of holy water in their pious practices; however, these two men, at least, clearly did not.[9] The laity, at least those in the Forest of Dean, actively engaged in both discussions and actions related to the promotion of Protestantism, thanks to Bishop Latimer and his preachers.

The First Act for the Dissolution of the Monasteries was promulgated in 1536. The immediate result was the dismembering and physical destruction of the smaller monasteries all over England. The buildings held by most monasteries dissolved by this act quickly became veritable quarries, where wealthy landholders could acquire lovely carved architectural enhancements for their private homes. Additionally, local elite members of society could purchase lands previously held by monasteries and thus enhance their own wealth, since in this time, land was wealth. However, the dissolution of the monasteries was less—much less—about religion than it was about the accumulation of wealth by the Crown. The primary beneficiary of the dissolution process was the king, who was looking for a source of funds for his anticipated war with France, a war that never came. That being said, the dissolution dealt a devastating blow to traditional religion, eliminating in short order pilgrimage sites, sources of hospitality for those in need, and institutions whose inhabitants often devoted much of their time and energy to praying for the dead. Additionally,

9. HWRO, 802 BA 2764, 172.

monks and nuns still had to be supported, if inadequately, by the Crown, diminishing the amount of wealth that could be accumulated by the king from this endeavor.

This First Act for the Dissolution of the Monasteries prompted an immediate response in the north of England in the form of the Pilgrimage of Grace. Once again lay people were attempting to insert themselves into the creation of religious policy in England. Those involved in this uprising demanded that the monasteries be restored, that Cromwell be punished, and that "heretical" bishops be deposed. This was an uprising that began in October 1536 in Lincolnshire but quickly spread to Yorkshire, where approximately thirty thousand men were assembled under the leadership of Robert Aske. England had no standing army at the time, and Henry VIII was unable to assemble a force of nearly that size. Therefore, after just a couple of months, the king negotiated a peace, acceded to the demands of the uprising, and offered a full pardon to those involved. Believing they had achieved their goals, those involved in the uprising disbanded and returned to their homes. However, a short time later, the king reneged on his promises, executed the leaders of the uprising, and continued the process of dissolving the monasteries. The Pilgrimage of Grace had failed. There would not be another uprising in Henry VIII's reign.

A second act targeting the larger monasteries would follow a few years later.[10] Tewkesbury in Gloucestershire was one of the monasteries dissolved by the second of these acts, and this resulted in the town purchasing the Abbey Church from the Crown for £483. The impetus for this came from the fact that the parish had worshipped in the nave of the church for a very long time ("since time out of mind," in the parlance of the day). This purchase, which remarkably

10. *L&P*, vol. XII, part I, nos. 308, 831; Baskerville, "The Dispossessed Religious of Gloucestershire," 130–44.

saved nearly the entire building, enabled the parish to continue to worship in that space. Only a few other abbeys, including Christchurch in Devon and Wymondham in Norfolk, were purchased by their towns. Meanwhile those in Malmesbury, Bolton, and Pershore were purchased by parishioners or patrons.[11]

The Royal Injunctions of 1536 discouraged superstitious beliefs concerning pilgrimages, relics, and images, and required that each church purchase a Bible and the *Paraphrases* (of the Gospels) in English by Desiderius Erasmus. Also, the clergy were to teach the Lord's Prayer, the Creed, and the Ten Commandments in English to their parishioners. The Injunctions issued two years later ordered the removal of images, the keeping of a record of baptisms, marriages, and burials in a parish register (a document still in use today), and (again) the placing in churches of a large Bible in English. Furthermore, all lay men and elite lay women were to be encouraged to read this Bible. That being said, the repeated requirement that an English Bible be acquired indicates that most parishes had not yet made this purchase, perhaps because of the cost. Bibles were expensive—paper was expensive, and the printing process was laborious. However, printing was an indispensable tool in support of the spread of Protestantism. It was, after all, "a religion of the book," so it needed books.[12] Thus, Royal Injunctions that included requirements for making English Bibles available and promoting the reading of them by the laity were used to begin to change religious policy in England in the 1530s.[13] Through these Injunctions, the

11. GRO Tewkesbury Borough Records B2/1, fo. 1; Knowles, *The Religious Orders of England, vol. III,* 384–86.

12. MacCulloch, *The Reformation,* 72.

13. "The First Royal Injunction of Henry VIII," in *VAI,* vol. II, 9; "The Second Royal Injunctions of Henry VIII," in *VAI,* vol. II, 38.

laity were encouraged to study the Scriptures thoroughly, an important aspect of Protestantism.

Once those in power had taken steps to break with the Church in Rome and to introduce some aspects of Lutheran theology in England, some clergy who supported these changes, like Thomas Cranmer and Hugh Latimer, gained new levels of authority and licensed like-minded preachers. Ordinary people responded to these developments in different ways. Some welcomed the new faith, including those in the Forest of Dean who gathered privately to discuss theology or demonstrated their new-found beliefs publicly. These people, and others in other places, were re-examining their faith—re-shaping their personal religious identities.

However, while Protestantism may have been welcomed by some people, and the king may have inadvertently helped its spread, throughout the 1520s and 1530s, and even into the 1540s, the old religion continued to thrive. The people continued in their traditional personal pious practices and attended Mass with their rosaries in hand. Where there was wealth, as in the areas noted for their wool production and wealthy wool merchants, the people continued to rebuild and refurbish their churches. Numerous churches in both the Cotswolds and East Anglia had been rebuilt in the latest perpendicular style from the ground up in the previous decades, attesting to the continuing vitality of traditional religion. Both the Cambridgeshire church of St. Wendreda's in March and the East Anglian church of St. Mary's in Bury St. Edmund's boasted of an elaborate double hammer-beam ceiling festooned with carved wooden angels. In Cirencester (in Gloucester), the people were just putting the finishing touches on their newest chantry chapels (where a priest would offer prayers for the dead, day and night), right up to the time of the death of Henry VIII early in 1547. More generally, parishioners refurbished church interiors, at least in minor ways, when they could afford the cost.

Some religious leaders in England may have hoped (or feared), that the efforts of Queen Anne, Cromwell, and Cranmer, plus eloquent and persuasive preachers, such as Bishop Hugh Latimer and his string of preachers, would lead to Protestantism sweeping across England under Henry VIII's authority, but that would not prove to be the case. The advance of Protestantism was neither widespread nor celebrated among the majority of the laity. At the monarchical level, Henry may have read the books Anne Boleyn urged him to read, including at least one by William Tyndale, and he may have initially turned a blind eye to the furtherance of Lutheran ideas in the early 1530s. However, he would still leave a very traditional will reflecting his Catholic beliefs.

By the end of the 1530s, there were pockets of Protestantism throughout southern England but mainly in Worcestershire and Gloucestershire where Latimer was bishop, and in London and East Anglia, areas closely tied to the continent through the wool trade. In other areas in the north and the west, and even in specific regions within those areas just mentioned, the traditional faith was still the preference of most.

CONSERVATIVE RESURGENCE

By the late-1530s, Henry VIII, along with members of his Privy Council and other powerful men in England, began working to curtail the spread of Protestant beliefs, by passing laws to outlaw them and reaffirm traditional beliefs and actions. These actions were welcomed by most. Members of local churches were comforted and reassured by the continuation of familiar religious practices. Customary piety continued to enrich the lives of its adherents, and at the highest levels of the realm the continuation of traditional religion was encouraged. Parishioners relied on traditional piety in familiar worship spaces for spiritual nurture. They didn't want to change. In fact, at multiple levels they resisted change.

At the end of this decade, in 1539, Parliament passed the Act of Six Articles. Disavowing several key theological assertions of burgeoning Protestantism, this act was inspired by the desire among conservative nobles and some ecclesiastical leaders to stem the tide of Protestantism and return religious policy to its earlier traditional form. Among these leaders, the time for compromise was over. Conservatives had gained the ascendancy. This Act included the following provisions:

- The doctrine of transubstantiation would (once again) be the eucharistic doctrine of the Church in England.

- Communion in both kinds was not necessary for the laity. (It was sufficient for them to receive the communion wafer only, not the wine.)

- Priests were not to marry.

- Vows of chastity or widowhood by men and women were to be observed and respected.

- Private Masses were acceptable.

- Private confession was acceptable.

The Act also included severe penalties for denying these articles and asserted that all but the last article were ordained by God. This Act effectively put the brakes on the surge of Protestantism across the realm.[14] This backlash came to dominate religious policy through the rest of Henry's reign.

14. 31 Henry VIII, c.14.

The Church in England during this time has been described as embodying Henrician Catholicism: Catholicism without a pope. However, that is an over-simplification. Thomas Cranmer was still archbishop of Canterbury, after all. Writing special liturgies in English, as Cranmer did during this time, was definitely not in line with Catholic doctrine. The efforts to eradicate Protestantism totally and replace it completely with true Catholicism (even without the pope) were unsuccessful. This was also evident in the fact that Henry's last wife, the learned Katherine Parr, controlled the education of two of his successors, Edward VI and Elizabeth I. This education was humanist in nature and not at all hostile to Protestantism.

Two separate actions by the conservative Privy Council of Henry VIII that focused on leaders of the Protestant effort illustrate the complexity of Henrician religion. Thomas Cromwell, the king's secretary, was the son of a blacksmith who had risen above his station to be one of the most powerful men in England. Inspired by Martin Luther and other continental reformers, he also became one of the architects of the emerging Protestant Church in England, as noted earlier. The dissolution of the monasteries in the second half of the 1530s, of which he was the architect, may have been the last straw for those with strong ties to Catholicism. As a man who had risen so far and tried to eradicate the revered religion of so many, including key powerful people, his death was probably inevitable. He was executed on July 28, 1540.

Cromwell's fellow reformer, Archbishop Thomas Cranmer, was more fortunate. His marriage (which violated Church law, since Cranmer was a priest) had become public knowledge, at least among the elite. Henry certainly knew. In 1543, Cranmer received a letter summoning him to a meeting of the Privy Council, a meeting of which he had not been aware, despite being a member of that august body. Interestingly, the king knew he had been summoned and arranged to meet with him before he presented himself to the Council. Henry told him what was about to happen and gave him his favorite ring, to signal to the Council that Cranmer had his support. When Cranmer arrived, the councilors placed him under arrest. Then he laid the ring on the table. Their plan was thwarted by the king, and they knew it. Cranmer left the meeting to return the ring to the king. He would continue to influence English religious policy through the rest of the reigns of both Henry VIII and Edward VI.[15]

Meanwhile, reforming bishops, such as Hugh Latimer, were replaced and chose to go into exile on the continent, along with numerous clergy (including John Hooper, the future bishop of Gloucester). Additionally, inhabitants of the Forest of Dean were brought before the Church courts to answer for their words and actions challenging the traditional faith. Traditional religion flourished. Some churches enhanced their buildings with accoutrements of conventional worship. Practices that had been frowned upon during the previous decade, such as private masses and private confession, were once again encouraged.

At the same time, lay testators continued to leave wills articulating their traditional faith. As discussed in the introduction, wills usually included three bequests: of the soul, of the body, and of worldly goods, and testators typically relied on scribes to prepare their wills, including their soul bequests or will preambles. Traditionally, testators bequeathed their souls to "Almighty God, the Blessed Virgin Mary, and the whole Company of Heaven." However, testators now wanted to elaborate on their beliefs in their bequests, including more detail and articulating a

15. MacCulloch, *Cranmer*, 320–21.

more Christ-centered faith. For instance, one man left his soul to God's mercy, "desiring and trusting that it may have the fruition of his [Christ's] glory with our Blessed Lady Saint Mary and all the holy company of heaven."[16] Others invoked the Holy Trinity. Proportionately, traditional will preambles were the most frequently used during this period. However, a substantial number also bequeathed their souls to "Almighty God," period, a totally ambiguous dedication.

While support for traditional religion was evident in policies as well as wills, it was not the only religious policy being implemented. Protestant policies were still being introduced, if only incrementally and even subtly. In fact, Cranmer's success when confronting the Privy Council, underscored by the continued support he received from the king, resulted in his quietly pushing ahead with some reforms, most notable in liturgy. In 1544, as Henry was preparing to go into battle against the French, he asked Cranmer to prepare a Litany of prayers in support of his war efforts, as was traditionally done in England. Cranmer complied, but he wrote this in English! It would be the first of many liturgies in English. Additionally, in keeping with Protestant theology, it provided no opportunity for invocations of the saints or other such traditional pious practices.

King Henry VIII died on January 28, 1547. His will was traditional in its pious provisions; however, it was a bit problematic regarding the succession. Henry was succeeded by his only male heir, Edward VI, age nine. Therefore, Henry named a Council of Regency comprised of sixteen executors, an unwieldy number, to serve until Edward reached the age of eighteen. His choice of Council members further illustrates the somewhat ambiguous nature of his faith. Yes, he had supported the introduction of more

16. GRO Gloucestershire Wills 1545/331.

conservative religious policies in his last years. However, he made sure one of the most powerful of the conservative clergy, Stephen Gardiner, the bishop of Winchester, was not included in the Council. That body, in turn, chose Edward Seymour, Edward VI's uncle, to serve as Lord Protector during the regency, rather than governing as a Council during that time. This would work for a while, but then disagreements over the pace and nature of religious change, as well as economic strain and military struggles, would lead to Seymour's downfall. He would be replaced by John Dudley, the Duke of Northumberland. However, these changes at the top during the next reign, would not slow the movement toward Protestantism.

DISCUSSION QUESTIONS

1. How do you think students' reading and discussing Lutheran books in university towns in England influenced the spread of Protestantism across England?

2. How was it that people in remote areas of England, like the Forest of Dean, came to espouse radical Protestant ideas?

3. What specific gifts and actions made Thomas Cromwell so influential in the initial spread Protestantism in England in the 1530s? What led to his demise?

4. How did Ann Boleyn become more than just the second wife of King Henry VIII?

3

ENGLAND BECOMES OFFICIALLY PROTESTANT

(1547–53)

Henry VIII was succeeded as king by his nine-year-old son, Edward VI, a fervent follower of John Calvin, the second-generation leader of Swiss Reform. This was in contrast to the English Protestantism of the 1530s, which was largely informed by Luther's theology. The difference was two-fold. First, Calvin's predecessor Ulrich Zwingli and his followers had looked back to the past event of the crucifixion as they commemorated the Last Supper, thinking of it primarily as a memorial. By contrast, followers of Luther stayed in the present moment. For that is when Luther's followers believed the body and the blood of Jesus became present with the bread and wine. In a different way, Calvin too stayed in the present moment, believing that Christ was *spiritually* present in the Eucharist. This is the position Cranmer would embrace before the end of Edward VI's reign. Second, there was a difference in the perception of images: were they merely benign "poor peoples' books," or were they dangerous idols that could draw people into worshipping them, which would doom those people to hell? Those embracing Swiss Reform—both that of Zwingli and that of Calvin—believed the latter. Luther's followers believed the former. Whether influenced by Luther or by either Zwingli's or Calvin's version of Swiss Reform, with Edward's accession, the archbishop of Canterbury, Thomas Cranmer, was given a free hand to orchestrate the introduction of true Protestantism into England.

This chapter will respond to several of the questions initially posed in the introduction. In the discussion of the first two *Books of Common Prayer*, this chapter will contribute to the story of the origins of the Church of England. Additionally, it will shed further light on the role of the laity in the religious changes in England in the sixteenth century and fill in much of the answer to the question of why the English Church looks the way it does.

Cranmer began slowly (from his perspective, that is). He believed that the way to effect this change was by changing worship, and he wanted to make such changes gradually. The first step was a set of Visitation Articles and Injunctions that focused on reforming the worship space. Then, through the rest of Edward's reign, more and more changes in worship itself were introduced to change the religion of the people. He introduced *The Order for Communion in Both Kinds* (that is, both bread and wine), which would be used during the distribution of the bread and wine to the people, and which also included a General Confession in English (which was to be used in place of private confession, a practice that was being discouraged).[1] Next came the first *Book of Common Prayer* with its modest changes to both the language and rubrics of worship. Then came the much more radically Protestant second *Prayer Book*, which changed the language of the liturgy, eliminated the invocation of the Holy Spirit in the Eucharist, and prohibited colorful vestments, images, and making the sign of the cross, among other restrictions.

Meanwhile, from the viewpoint of parish leaders and parishioners, the changes were sudden and dramatic. Just imagine the shock of hearing the Mass proclaimed in the English language, or the altar replaced by a Communion table positioned in the center aisle of the nave, or (later on) the priest leading worship dressed in the black and white of cassock and surplice, rather than a colorful chasuble or cope over a white alb! The evidence available indicates that neither the gradual changes in the liturgy nor the more startling changes in the language and absence of images within the worship space resulted in an acceptance of Protestantism. Rather, for the most part the people clung to their traditional faith. For them, the changes came too fast and pushed too far. This is clear from the evidence in the Church courts, in churchwardens' accounts (showing how parishes spent their money), and in the wills of the people.

EARLY STEPS TOWARD PROTESTANTISM

Religious change had actually begun while Henry VIII was still alive, when in 1544 (as noted earlier) Cranmer had written a new litany in English. Worshipping in English was a key aspect of Protestant beliefs and a goal of reform,

1. *Order of Communion*, 1548.

along with hearing and reading Scriptures in the language of the people. Leaders of reform agreed. The laity needed to engage directly with the Word. The new litany was a step in the English process of reform and anticipated the additional changes to come during Edward's reign.

The Royal Visitation of 1547 was the next step toward reform, coming shortly after Edward became king. Notably, priests were now allowed to marry as a result of these Visitation Articles. However, this Visitation focused primarily on changing the worship spaces to eliminate "all superstition and hypocrisy, [that had] crept into diverse men's hearts" and their churches. More specifically, these Visitation Articles and Injunctions called for the removal of images of saints that had served as the object of pilgrimages and donations. They also prohibited the invocation of saints and the presence of torches, candles, tapers, or images of wax before any statue or picture of a saint. One specific injunction called for the removal of all shrines, "all tables, candlesticks, . . . rolls of wax, pictures, paintings, and all other monuments of feigned miracles, pilgrimages, idolatry, and superstition," so that there remained no memory "of the same in walls, glass-windows, or elsewhere within their churches or houses." Notably, such images were to be removed from their domestic settings in peoples' houses, as well as from churches. The Visitation Article calling for the removal of images painted on the walls led churchwardens to hire painters to apply whitewash over the prohibited images. Furthermore, in some parishes, artists were also hired to write on the walls, typically replacing images with the words of the Lord's Prayer and the Ten Commandments.[2]

Having called for the removal, or replacement, of things deemed superstitious, these Injunctions went on to call for the addition (if the church did not already have one)

2. *VAI,* vol. II, eds, Frere and Kennedy, 103–30.

of "a comely and honest pulpit, to be set in a convenient place within the same, for the preaching of God's word." This pulpit, as had been the case with the requirement that each parish acquire the Bible in English and that images be obliterated, was to be paid for by the parish. Religious change did indeed place a financial strain on most parishes. Churchwardens had to pay for repairs to the building in the normal course of things, but additionally they might have had to fund installation of the pulpit and the acquisition of the English Bible, among other items. Some parishes chose to forego repairs to their buildings, while others opted to make needed repairs and ignored (or delayed responding to) the requirements of these Injunctions. Many simply could not afford any of these expenses or maybe didn't want to make such investments. All these changes in the worship space affected how the churches in England looked.

Although not mentioned in the Royal Injunctions of 1547, England's chantry chapels were also a target of reformers. They had been erected to provide spaces for Masses dedicated to praying for the dead. However, Protestantism judged such prayers to be superstitious, dangerous to laypeople's spiritual health, and based on erroneous beliefs concerning purgatory. Purgatory, according to traditional religion, was a place where people's souls resided while being cleansed of sin before entering heaven. This cleansing came through the peoples' record of their own good works and those of others, including prayers. This is where chantry priests came in.

Chantries had been funded over the years by endowments of land and valuable possessions, potential future sources of wealth for the Crown. Here religious change converged with the Crown's need for money. Protestants wanted to eliminate prayers for the dead. Confiscation of chantry endowments would benefit the Crown, while it would cripple these chantries financially and lead to their dissolution. Their elimination would remove a key source of prayers for the dead and send a message to others about the need to stop such practices. Henry VIII had taken the initial steps to confiscate the funds for these chantries with an act to inventory chantry endowments approved by Parliament in 1546, but he had not completed the process. Following the accession of the new king in 1547, a new Chantries Act was passed. However, the chantries would not actually be dissolved until later in Edward's reign when a more radical form of Protestantism characterized official religious policy across the realm.

Cranmer was indeed managing religious change across England. However, the resulting policies did not initially have a good outcome. In some places, a few people, probably influenced by Swiss reform, thought that change was not coming fast enough. They took advantage of the first steps toward Protestantism in Edward's reign but went much further, knocking down religious images in public squares and such. The destruction of images may have been motivated by a desire to protect their neighbors from worshipping these as idols and then being doomed to hell, but such actions violated established religious policy. Cranmer believed it had to be stopped. This resulted in the passage of the "Act against Revilers and for the Administration of the Sacrament in Both Kinds" in 1547.[3] This act combined two very different actions: the punishment of people who disrupted worship services or destroyed images; and the introduction of the new liturgy for distributing both the bread and wine to parishioners (*The Order of Communion in Both Kinds*, mentioned earlier).

Religious change continued with the introduction of additional aspects of Protestantism. Cranmer took charge

3. 1 Edward VI, c. 1.

of the preaching across the realm, publishing the *Book of Homilies* in 1547. Churches were required to purchase this book, and priests were required to read from it, rather than preaching their own sermons. This allowed the archbishop to control utterances from English pulpits in a way that would promote the new religion of the realm with some consistency. A select group of priests who already supported Protestantism had been licensed by the king to preach, but the vast majority were required to read their sermons from the approved homilies. These are what the people would hear. The content of sermons changed and contributed to the emerging image of the Church of England. Changes in the Catholic Mass and restrictions in traditional pious practices would also influence the way the Church looked. The creation of the two *Prayer Books* would change it more directly.

Ever so gradually, Cranmer was changing English worship. At least, he perceived these changes as gradual. The peoples' perception may have been different. Hearing any part of the liturgy in English could well have been jarring to ordinary parishioners used to the quiet celebration of the Mass in Latin. During the traditional Mass, the congregation participated either silently or in a low murmur of prayer, presumably, while the celebrant spoke so quietly that he might as well have been silent. However, this silence was interrupted by the ringing of a bell in anticipation of the time the priest would do something to which parishioners were expected to respond. The most significant of these times was when the priest elevated the eucharistic host, so that parishioners could see it from their pews. Lay people would hear the bell from their fields, workshops, and houses. They would drop everything and run into the church to kneel down and adore the host. If they were already in the church, they would have been reciting certain specified prayers in harmony with the actions of the presiding priest.

(These prayers were included in books called "Primers" that were memorized and repeated from memory by pious parishioners.) Lay participation may have varied a bit, depending on whether it was a Sunday, or a weekday, Mass, or on the parish where they resided, but there was always participation, and it was familiar.[4] The English-language *Order of Communion* would have been a jarring interruption in this most sacred part of this traditional liturgy, and that would have been at least unsettling.

THE FIRST BOOK OF COMMON PRAYER (1549)

The next step in Cranmer's introduction of Protestantism came with the publication of the first *Book of Common Prayer*. On Whitsunday (Pentecost, June 9, 1549), the people arrived at their parish church as usual, but what they experienced there that morning was anything but "usual." When their priest spoke, he spoke in English and parishioners could hear him! In fact, the whole service was in English! Cranmer believed he was continuing to introduce change gradually, and indeed, a careful reader could find portions of the traditional Sarum Mass, albeit in an English translation of the original Latin, in the liturgy of Holy Communion. However, most may not have noticed. Rather, they would probably have been shocked that the priest spoke in English, and that he did not elevate the Communion bread (the "host"), during the Prayer of Consecration. Cranmer was particularly determined to eliminate this practice, so that people no longer gazed upon the Communion host as if it were an idol. He was offended by the way people had run "from their seats to the altar, and from altar to altar

---

4. Duffy, *The Stripping of the Altars*, 92–130.

[in their church], . . . peeping, tooting, and gazing at that thing that the priest held up in his hands."[5] Hence, the priest was forbidden to raise it up. Additionally, all prayers for the dead were eliminated. All this being said, the main impact on the people would have been that the service was now in English, not Latin.[6] They may not have noticed some of the details of the other changes.

This *Prayer Book* also included other services (in English). A new set of Daily Offices, Morning and Evening Prayer, were among these. These liturgies were intended to replace the nine daily services used by monks and nuns before the dissolution of the monasteries, but they were now intended for use in parish churches. They were the result of a collaboration between clergy and scholars from various countries in Europe. Across Europe, by the early sixteenth century, few monks or nuns still said all nine of the required daily services. This led to the effort to consolidate them into just two services. Thomas Cranmer was a part of this effort and used the resulting liturgies as a basis for Morning and Evening Prayer in his new *Prayer Book*.[7] In these, as in the other liturgies included in this book, Cranmer's gifted use of the evolving English language is evident. Additionally, both services were soon used regularly. Frequent participation in Holy Communion was promoted in the *Prayer Book*, but it seldom happened. Rather, the Daily Offices, namely Morning Prayer (also called Matins), and Evening Prayer, soon became the principal services on Sundays.

The liturgies were also augmented. For instance, the Scriptures gained new prominence in the Holy Communion service, in that this service called for multiple passages

5. Cranmer, *Remains*, 442.

6. Cuming, *A History of Anglican Liturgy*, 47; *Prayer Books*, 1–317.

7 Here and in future instances in this work, *The Book of Common Prayer* is sometimes referred to as the *Prayer Book*.

from Scripture to be read. It included an Old Testament reading, a New Testament reading, and a reading from one of the Gospels, as well as a psalm. Similarly, each of the Daily Offices included two readings, one of which was to be from the Gospels, plus one or more psalms. Additionally, Gospel-based preaching, which in most cases took the form of the reading of a sermon from the *Book of Homilies*, was to be included in all services offered on Sundays. The reading of more passages from Scripture in worship services underscored the importance of the Bible in England, as well as on the continent. However, there was more.

The *Prayer Book* liturgies also provided for lay participation in the form of audible responses to the priest's words. Initially these responses would have been uttered by the parish clerk on behalf of the congregation. He was, in most cases, one of the few members of the parish who could read, and most churches could only afford a maximum of two copies of this book: one for the priest and one for the parish clerk. Probably, the expectation was that the rest of the congregation would soon learn these responses by memorizing what the parish clerk repeated each Sunday. In congregations that conscientiously conformed to this new form of worship, that is probably what happened. (When few people can read, memorization is easy.) In the traditional Church, as noted earlier, the laity had participated silently, or at least quietly, during the Mass, reciting their own prayers. With the advent of Protestant worship, lay responses were peppered throughout the liturgies; audibility was key.

RESISTANCE TO THE FIRST PRAYER BOOK

This first *Prayer Book* was the last straw for some of those who preferred traditional religion. Protests, and even armed uprisings fueled by both religious change and worsening economic conditions became a very real threat in many communities. Interestingly, complaints from those in Cornwall asserted that worshipping in English, where people typically spoke Cornish and didn't understand English, was no better than a service in Latin. Further, they resented the religious change signaled by the liturgy being in English. They preferred the old familiar religion. This was also true in Norfolk, where the Duke of Norfolk was a powerful supporter of traditional religion. This resistance would eventually result in general disorder and even regional rebellions in both Cornwall and Norfolk after the introduction of the first *Prayer Book*. These uprisings targeted the new religion and the authorities who were promoting it. In short order, they led to the downfall of the Duke of Somerset as lord protector and the ascendancy of the Duke of Northumberland, ruling in the name of King Edward VI. However, the change at the top did not change the overall trajectory of religious change, all of which would contribute to the creation of the form of worship and the space where it took place seen in the Church of England and other Anglican and Episcopal churches today.

MORE RELIGIOUS CHANGE BETWEEN PRAYER BOOKS

At the highest levels in the realm, religious policy continued to change during the early 1550s. Those representing the Crown rediscovered the Chantries Act of 1547, leading to attempts to seize all Church goods (including all endowments) documented in the survey of 1546. However, this effort was only partially successful, as many assets were hidden or had been sold to others. The completion of a revised version of the *Prayer Book*, reflecting the increased influence of Swiss Reform, was more successful. The Reformation in England was still being influenced by those on the continent.

From the publication of the first *Prayer Book*, worship had continued to evolve. In the Diocese of Gloucester, Bishop Hooper called for altars in parish churches to be lowered to the level of the pews in the nave where parishioners sat. To do so, compliant churchwardens hired workers to remove the dirt from under the chancel floor and the area where the altar was located, since the floors in churches were typically composed of paving stones laid on top of the dirt.[8] Similarly, across the realm parishes paid to have rood lofts removed. These were lofts or beams that stretched across the chancel arch, displaying a crucifix in the center, flanked by statues of the Blessed Virgin Mary and the disciple, John. This image-laden loft marked the boundary between the nave where worshippers sat and the chancel and sanctuary, occupied by the worship leaders, including the priest or priests and possibly the parish choir. The worship space was thus transformed. The images were removed, and the delineation of the chancel and sanctuary from the nave was essentially eliminated. The laity now had a clear view of the presiding priest and any others involved in leading worship. Additionally, lay responses joined with the priest's utterances to form a conversation of sorts that flowed unhindered between the nave and the chancel.

Such changes may have been typical in London under Bishop Ridley, as well as in Gloucestershire, but they were not the norm across the realm. True, in many parishes in England, traditional, "superstitious" practices such as using ashes on Ash Wednesday and palms on Palm Sunday, "creeping to the cross" on Good Friday, and erecting an Easter Sepulcher on Holy Saturday may have long since been

8. GRO, St. Michael's Accounts, P154/14 CW 1/5.

abolished. However, conforming to Protestant changes and prohibitions was not all that common. Traditional practices in worship and personal piety had not vanished from the realm. Some congregations and individuals continued with their "old ways," defying the authorities. Surreptitiously, for instance, some individuals still prayed the rosary, at least at home and sometimes even in churches. And in many places, the priest chose to continue to say the liturgy of Holy Communion, especially the Prayer of Consecration, in a whisper, as he had when the service was in Latin. In this way, he could effectively hide the fact that the service was in English and the theology had changed. He also might have ignored the prohibition against elevating the communion host. Who would report him? In most cases, no one. In most cases, parishes seem to have been united in their desire either for reform or for continuing with traditional, familiar practices in worship, and many, probably a majority, preferred the old way over the new. When the visitors sent by an official Visitation inquired, the churchwardens could say they had nothing to report and know that, in most cases, parishioners would stay silent. Such unanimity was a powerful tool in keeping secret any deviations from established religious policy.

However, not all parishes were in agreement in their response to official religious policy. Across the realm, contention ensued in some parishes, even in parishes where the priest was very, very clear about his position. Hadleigh in Suffolk (in the Diocese of Norwich), with its rector, Rowland Taylor, and Tudenham in Gloucester, with its vicar, Sir William Living, are two examples of this. Both priests favored Protestant reform to one degree or another. Taylor was a protégé of Cranmer and shared the archbishop's approach to reform. In Edward's reign, he disposed of many of the accoutrements of traditional worship, including church plate (chalices and such), vestments, and bells. However, some things survived this cleansing. He kept the organ and even refurbished it, along with the Easter sepulcher, with its "light" or taper (which had been ordered removed in some dioceses) was used at Easter. (Followers of Swiss Reform viewed organs and candles or tapers as sources of idolatry, so they stopped using them and let them fall into disrepair.) Perhaps, in Hadleigh, this was a compromise with parish leaders like the brothers John and Walter Clerke, who bequeathed their souls in the traditional manner to "Almighty God and to his blessed mother Saint Mary the Virgin and to all the angels and archangels in heaven." Both men were clothiers of wealth and standing. They were joined by Henry Constable and John Ellice, husbandmen who also left traditional wills.[9] So, members of congregations sometimes resisted the innovations made to create a more Protestant Church of England. However, in some cases the laity, with or without the local clergy, acted in ways that got ahead of official Protestant policy.

In Tudenham, the vicar, Sir William Living, seems to have been at odds with the majority of his congregation, most of whom continued in their traditional faith. Living, on the other hand, was a radical Protestant influenced by Swiss Reform. Members of his congregation accused him of breaking glass windows in the church that contained images and of no longer saying Mass. Also, he and a parishioner were accused of knocking down a cross in the churchyard.[10]

While the people were struggling to define their faith in light of official religious policy, the Crown was also initiating a process to revise Canon Law (that is Church law), to reflect that official policy. On November 11, 1551, Edward VI appointed thirty-two men, including Archbishop

9. Craig, "Reformers, Conflict, and Revisionism," 19–20.
10. GRO Gloucester Borough Records, vol. IV, 55.

Cranmer as chair, to prepare a new set of Canon Laws. Up to this point, since Henry VIII's break with Rome, the ecclesiastical hierarchy had been using a modified version of Roman Canon Law to regulate the Church and moral behavior in England. This project was completed in March 1553; however, the king was too ill by then to push for approval by Parliament. England would not have its own set of Canon Laws until after James VI & I became king, following Elizabeth I's death some fifty years later.[11]

THE SECOND BOOK OF COMMON PRAYER (1552)

Cranmer's religious policy continued to evolve. He was still in charge, despite challenges from both those who thought he was not moving fast enough and those who thought he was introducing change much too rapidly. On All Saints Sunday, the first Sunday in November, in 1552 (which was November second that year) parishioners were shocked anew. A new *Book of Common Prayer* was introduced across England on that date, and as with the first *Prayer Book*, this book was used in most parishes on that Sunday and beyond.[12] Parish priests now were dressed in black and white—cassock and surplice. Worship had been stripped of all remaining facets that engaged the senses, such as color and smell. In terms of color, in conforming parishes not only was there no color in the priest's vestments, but more and more parishes had no color on the walls, just whitewash.

Instead of the traditional altar positioned against the east wall of the worship space, a trestle table was positioned with the small ends toward the east and west, either between

11 *"Reformatium Legum Ecclessiiasticarum,"* 166–69.

12. *Prayer Books*, 319–404; Hutton, "Local Impact" 125.

the opposable choir pews in the chancel or in the center aisle in the nave. The priest stood on the north (left from the congregation's perspective) side of this table when he presided. Also, the words of worship had been edited to ensure they reflected the truth contained in the Scriptures, according to the judgment of Cranmer and other Church leaders in England. Hence, the invocation of the Holy Spirit during the consecration of the bread and wine in the Communion service had been eliminated, as had the blessing of the water of baptism. Similarly, priests no longer made the sign of the cross at any point in any liturgy. That action had been prohibited. With worship stripped to its bare essentials after the publication of this second *Prayer Book*, parishes sold books, vestments, and other items that were no longer needed. At St. Michael's in Gloucester the receipts totaled £27.[13]

The service of Holy Communion began in both the 1549 and 1552 books with the Collect for Purity—"Almighty God, unto whom all hearts are open, . . ."—as has been true in each *Prayer Book* developed since. In 1552, this prayer was followed by the Ten Commandments, which in the previous few years had emerged as a replacement for penance for people who had been found guilty by the Church courts. When the Church court was sitting, this was the punishment chosen by the court several times each day. Those found guilty were to say the Ten Commandments and the Lord's Prayer (at least) on the following Sunday, while standing in front of their congregation. In addition, the Gloria had been moved to the end of the service since Cranmer believed it to be too joyful for the beginning of worship. Also, the Peace had been removed and the Prayer for the Whole State of Christ's Church added.

Perhaps most notably, the words of administration of the Communion elements were changed between 1549

13. GRO P154/14 CW 1/5.

and 1552. At this time, there were a number of different beliefs about the bread and wine of the Eucharist. The traditional belief of transubstantiation asserted that during the liturgy the bread and wine were actually, physically *turned into* the body and blood of Jesus Christ by the priest's words (a form of "real presence"). The bread and wine still looked, smelled, and tested like bread and wine, that is, they were not changed outwardly. However, they were invisibly transformed inwardly. Somewhat similarly, as noted earlier, followers of Luther believed Jesus's body and blood were actually, physically present with the bread and wine, but not because of the priest's words. This was another form of "real presence." Followers of Ulrich Zwingli believed that the Eucharist was a *commemoration* of the institution of Holy Communion in the Last Supper. Meanwhile, Cranmer believed that consecration transformed something ordinary (like bread or wine) into something holy, imbued with the spiritual presence of Christ (like the sacramental elements of the Eucharist), to feed the people of God spiritually. Thus, Cranmer believed in the *spiritual presence* of Christ in the bread and wine of the Eucharist, that as he swallowed the bread and wine of the Eucharist he was being fed spiritually by Christ.

In the first *Prayer Book*, the words for distributing the bread read, "The body of our Lord Jesus Christ given for thee, preserve thy body and soul unto everlasting life." Similar words were used with the wine. These words could be interpreted as supporting "real presence" and thus resonating with both traditional and Lutheran beliefs. In 1552, the words that accompanied the bread were "Take and eat this, in remembrance that Christ died for you, and feed on him in thy heart by faith, with thanksgiving." The words for the wine were nearly identical. These words were much more ambiguous, supporting beliefs in both spiritual presence and commemoration, but not any form of "real presence." This was a sign of the growing influence of Swiss Reform in England, as was the change in the rules for Communion bread. In 1549 the bread was to be plain wafers large enough to be broken into at least two pieces. In contrast, in 1552 according to the *Prayer Book*, the bread was to be the same as was eaten during a meal, to discourage believers even more clearly from seeing it as supporting any kind of "real presence."

From the introduction of this second *Prayer Book* to the end of Edward VI's reign in July 1553, official English religion was as radically Protestant as it would ever be. The liturgy had become more Protestant, more simplified than it would be in Anglican and Episcopal churches in the twenty-first century. More and more churches whitewashed their interiors to obliterate their wall paintings—their painted images. More and more churches modified the location and shape of their altar or Communion table and eliminated other now obsolete pieces of furniture from their worship space. At least some churches were becoming, essentially, auditoriums for the Word of God—for reading Scriptures and for preaching—but were also presenting a less-exalted site for Holy Communion. The placement of the Communion table in the midst of the choir or in the nave brought the sacred words and actions closer to the people, or at least suggested a more ordinary setting, almost like sharing a meal, but always still more than that.

EFFECT ON PERSONAL FAITH

Even though all these changes in religious policy did indeed bring radical Protestantism to England, it was not consistently implemented or accepted across the realm. Not all parishes conformed, either partially or completely, and the people did not necessarily welcome this radical Protestantism either, even when they were actually experiencing it. Wills from this time help us see this. As noted earlier, during this period there were three types of preambles to wills: traditional, ambiguous, and Protestant; and the use of ambiguous soul bequests soared, while the preference for traditional preambles nearly disappeared. Some did choose Protestant preambles, but the number was small.[14]

Bequeathing their souls to Almighty God, period (a totally ambiguous declaration), was far and away the most common expression of faith in wills written during Edward's reign. This clear majority of testators essentially ducked for cover, concealing their continuing traditional faith, or genuinely expressing the ambivalence of their faith in this time of great religious change. Some priests and bishops vigorously discouraged traditional soul bequests at this time, asserting that they were dangerous to the health of the testator's soul. Certainly, that was the message Bishop Hooper of the Diocese of Gloucester proclaimed—in his eyes, employing such preambles would be "injurious to God and perilous as well for the salvation of the dead."[15] However, as individual testators honestly examined their own faith, some still chose heartfelt traditional preambles for their wills. One courageous testator bequeathed her soul to "Almighty God, to our Lady and to the whole company of Heaven."[16] Few testators embraced Protestantism, even if those in authority did. However, there were some, and they were distinctive. One Joan Davis even adopted the entire first paragraph of William Tracy's will (from 1531), asserting

14. Litzenberger, *The English Reformation and the Laity*, 168–78.

15. "Bishop Hooper's Visitation Booke," Morice MS 31L, Item 3, 16.

16. GRO Gloucestershire Wills 1551/16.

> I commit me unto God and to his mercy trusting
> without any doubt or mistrust in his grace and
> the merits of Jesus Christ, and by the virtue of
> his passion and of his resurrection of body and
> soul: For I believe that my redeemer lives and in
> the last day I shall rise out of the earth and in my
> flesh shall see my savior. This my hope is laid up
> in my bosom.[17]

Less loquaciously, another testator who had embraced Protestantism bequeathed his soul "Into the merciful hands of Almighty God trusting without any doubt or mistrust that by the merits of Christ's passion that I have and shall [have] forgiveness of my sins."[18] The assuredness of salvation signaled by this declaration was a clear sign of Protestantism.

However, despite these eloquent examples, in Gloucestershire Protestant will preambles accounted for only about 5 percent annually of all such declarations by the end of Edward's reign, while traditional statements diminished throughout the reign to match the proportion of those aligned with the new religion. Most Edwardian wills—90 to 95 percent annually from the time of the first *Prayer Book* through the remainder of Edward's reign—included ambiguous will preambles. Given the Protestant religious policy of the realm, it is not surprising that those clinging to their traditional faith usually chose ambiguous soul bequests, as they strove to live in England without attracting attention. But why was this, really? Were they under pressure to conform with official religious policy? The evidence is not clear. However, many people seem to have believed they could be punished if they opted for traditional preambles. Or perhaps, they believed their bishops and priests when they argued

17. GRO Gloucestershire Wills 1551/62; Tyndale, "The Testament of Master William Tracy," 279.

18. GRO Gloucestershire Wills 1547/98.

against traditional statements of faith. Of course, it is also possible that testators may have been reeling from the speed of religious change and may not have been ready to embrace the new religion, at least not yet.

Elsewhere in England there was a similar proportion of traditional vs. Protestant will preambles. Yet, there were distinct Protestant will preambles prepared during Edward's reign. One Thomas Brounsmythe of Hadleigh, in his will dated late in December 1547, commended his soul unto "Christ Jesus, my maker and redeemer, by whom and by the merits of whose blessed passion is all my whole trust of clean remission and forgiveness of my sins." He continued, prohibiting dirges and directly his wife to find someone to preach a sermon instead. And he further insisted that the sermon "laud and praise my Lord and Savior Jesus Christ" and preach the Scriptures. Similarly, in 1549, John Myton of Shrewsbury declared, "The ground of my belief is that there is but one mediator between God and man, which man; as Paul saith, is Christ Jesus." Continuing in a similar vein to Brounsmyth, he forbade the use of dirges but requested "the Te Deum in English, and godly psalms, for the comfort and edifying of the people." He went on to condemn the Mass as something to be "abhorred of all those that professed Christ. For as Paul saith, Christ hath offered himself once for all."[19] However, there were not many such wills, distinctive or otherwise. Most of the people were not yet ready to embrace Protestantism. Each lay person's will was an indicator, not only of that testator's beliefs, but also of the degree to which each one would support or resist reform. Once again, lay beliefs, nuanced as they often were, helped create the diverse, yet united, church we know today.

---

19. Craig, "Reformers, Conflict, and Revisionism," 18–19; Coulton, "The Establishment of Protestantism," 309–10.

THE ABRUPT END OF EDWARDIAN PROTESTANTISM

Unfortunately, especially for those working for Protestant reform, Edward's reign did not last long enough for people to perceive its enriching aspects. He died on July 6, 1553, at the age of sixteen. He had not even reached his majority. His fervent hope that Protestantism inspired by John Calvin would be embraced by his subjects across the realm was unrealized. There had not been time for the acceptance of such great change.

DISCUSSION QUESTIONS

1. Why was it so hard for the leaders in England to gain acceptance of Protestantism from the people during Edward's reign?

2. Do you think it was wise of Thomas Cranmer to introduce Protestantism so gradually during Edward's reign?

3. Why was Cranmer's understanding of gradual change so at odds with the perspective of ordinary people who were shocked by worship prescribed by the first *Book of Common Prayer*?

4. How do you think English Protestantism would have been different if Edward had reigned longer, say for another twenty years? Why?

4

MARIAN CATHOLICISM REIGNS SUPREME

(1553–58)

EDWARD VI's DEATH, PROBABLY of tuberculosis, came as a shock to many, especially the Duke of Northumberland who had ruled in the later years for the boy king. The duke had been working behind the scenes to prevent Edward's eldest sister, Mary, daughter of Henry VIII and Catherine of Aragon, from claiming the throne. She had been a Catholic all her life, and yes, the religion of the monarch still determined the official religion of the realm. After six years of increasingly Protestant religious policy, England would now revert to a version of Catholicism labeled Marian Catholicism, but that would not happen without a fight, and the story of this is fascinating. In confronting the restoration of Catholicism, Protestants had choices. Elite

Protestant women found creative ways to resist the new religious policy and actively support those sentenced by the Crown to die as martyrs. The martyrs included prominent theologians, as well as women and boys, whose faith was so strong they felt they could do nothing but step forward to certain death. Their fate was inevitable. Others either concealed their faith or sought exile on the continent.

This chapter focuses primarily on Mary's efforts to reestablish Catholicism and the responses of Protestants to these changes in the religion of the realm. It also examines women's roles in promoting Protestantism and the process by which they develop their religious identities. In discussing these developments, it will also shed additional light on the ways both continental Catholic reform and other Protestant Reformations, particularly that in Switzerland, influenced English religion, and on the role of the laity in determining religious policy during Mary's reign and beyond.

THE RISE AND FALL OF LADY JANE GREY

Prior to his death, Edward, probably guided by Northumberland, had drafted the "Device for the Succession," by which they intended to thwart the terms of Henry VIII's will. The "Device" named Edward's cousin, Lady Jane Grey, the eldest daughter of Henry's younger sister, Mary, and the wife of Northumberland's son, as his heir. (There were no male candidates available.) Documents were prepared in June that bastardized both Mary and Elizabeth, Henry VIII's two surviving children. Then Parliament was summoned to give legislative force to the "Device." However,

Edward died too soon. Neither the "Device" nor the other documents had been approved.[1]

Northumberland was unprepared for the rapid demise of the young king and waited three days before proclaiming Lady Jane Grey to be the queen. Meanwhile Mary fled to Norfolk where she began mustering her forces. When she began her march south to claim the throne, she was greeted by a groundswell of popular support. People (even prominent Protestants like Bishop John Hooper of Gloucester) respected her legitimate claim. They hated Northumberland. By the time Mary reached London, her supporters had captured Northumberland and his associates, and put them in the Tower. It was August 3, 1553. Queen Jane had "ruled" for less than a month.

QUEEN MARY'S REIGN BEGINS

Mary's accession was the result of the failed attempts, over the previous twenty-five years, to save the realm from a female ruler. Mary was thirty-seven and unmarried. Her reign has been maligned for the way it tried to restore Catholicism. Some historians have labeled her "Bloody Mary" for her prosecution of Protestants as heretics and have suggested that all that bloodletting was for naught. However, she inherited some daunting challenges. These included an economic downturn, bad harvests, and the worst epidemic (influenza) since the Black Death in the fourteenth century. All this was in addition to her desire to return Catholicism to England. Her administration of her realm was, in fact, sound and her financial policies sensible in the face of the ongoing economic struggles the country was dealing with. She also took a methodical approach to returning

1. *Proclamation, 10 July 1553.*

Catholicism to England that could have succeeded. However, she did not have time to complete this process.

Marian Catholicism was all about boundaries: boundaries between acceptable Catholic beliefs and those deemed unacceptable or heretical. Motivated in part by her intense personal piety, Mary and her bishops moved swiftly to implement the restoration of a form of Catholicism to England. At first her policy seemed quite simple: restore the Mass and the other elements of traditional liturgy, including the worship space, to the way they were at the time of Henry VIII's death. This policy was introduced in a Royal Proclamation issued on August 18, 1553. This Proclamation, accompanied by a set of Injunctions, inhibited preaching, condemned the use of "newfound" terms, such as "papist" and "heretic," and predicted that a religious settlement would be worked out "by common consent." It also declared that priests would once again wear colorful vestments and the altar would be returned to the east wall above the level of the congregation. The rood loft with its "rood" or crucifix, flanked by statues of Mary and John, would once again fill the chancel arch. These injunctions also specified that choir voices would again fill the whole church with beautiful music during the Mass, and that parishioners would be surrounded by familiar images, like crucifixes and images of the Blessed Virgin Mary. (If a person had sung in the church choir in Edward's reign, when the service was in English, they were required to remain in the choir during Mary's reign, when the service was in Latin.)[2] As with Cranmer in Edward's reign, the focus was on changing worship.

However, by the first week of September things had changed, and Mary indicated to foreign ambassadors (who had positioned themselves as her advisors) that she intended

2. "Bonner's Articles," 351–52.

to restore the Church in England and Ireland to obedience to the papacy "as they were before the changes." That was a significantly more extreme restoration than those ambassadors had recommended. They had proposed merely a return to the Catholicism of the last years of Henry's reign, the policy outlined in her first Royal Proclamation.

The one prominent person who applauded Mary's decision to restore the authority of the pope in England was her cousin, Cardinal Reginald Pole, who had her ear. He requested and received from the pope a mission to England and the title of papal legate; he arrived in England about a year later in November 1554. Meanwhile, Mary realized (and her advisors urged) that she should go slowly regarding the papacy. There was much greater animosity toward the pope than toward the Mass in England. The Mass was restored in September 1553, and the peoples' acceptance of it was a welcome relief to Mary, illustrating another way the laity were involved in religious change in sixteenth-century England. Parishioners' return to Catholicism effectively stopped the Reformation in its tracks, if only for a few years.

Following England's initial return to Catholicism, Mary was inclined to ignore the Protestants, believing they would shrivel into insignificance. However, even before the Royal Proclamation was issued, it was clear that even within her household there were strong Protestant feelings (and those people weren't going to return willingly to the Catholic fold). Some Protestant-leaning clergy from across England, including Rowland Taylor, rector of Hadleigh, were soon imprisoned. Others arrested early on included the most prominent of the religious leaders of the previous reign: Archbishop Cranmer and Bishops Ridley, Latimer, and Hooper. They and many of their co-religionists, both lay and ordained, both male and female, were imprisoned over the next two years and held well into 1555 when, if they hadn't recanted, they were burned as heretics.

THE SEVERAL RESPONSES OF PROTESTANTS TO MARIAN RELIGIOUS POLICY

The clarity of the boundary between Catholicism and Protestantism in Mary's reign offered people the opportunity to examine and declare their faith both privately and publicly. Those who had embraced Protestantism during the previous reign soon realized that they had five options: (i) return to the traditional religion (Catholicism), (ii) choose martyrdom, (iii) choose exile, (iv) hide in plain sight in England, or (v) continue to gather and worship quietly as Protestants. The last of these options was rarely successful, although one group in London did continue at great risk to meet throughout Mary's reign.[3] Meanwhile, Protestants were urged by the Crown to recant and return to Catholicism. Those who did not do so had three remaining options: martyrdom, exile, or hiding in plain sight in England. Those who chose martyrdom, along with the leaders of reform during Edward's reign (who had no choice), were soon arrested and generally refused to recant.

The Marian restoration of Catholicism challenged those who were unwilling to recant their reformed faith. These included the martyrs and those who cared for them prior to their martyrdom. Confronted with the reality of the clearly defined boundaries between Protestantism and Catholicism, adherents of the new religion defined their religious selves with increasing clarity through their words and their actions. Thus, from the beginning of Mary's reign

3. Dickens, *The English Reformation*, 273–75.

and the restoration of Catholicism, many of those who had embraced Protestantism during Edward's reign found their faith challenged and wanted to clarify it. They discovered and refined their religious identities, learning more precisely where the boundaries were in terms of their beliefs and practices. As a result, they were increasingly able to choose how best to respond to the policies of Marian Catholicism, and some individuals' faith may have been strengthened.

The Crown was determined to enforce its Catholic religious policies to achieve doctrinal conformity and eliminate heresy (that is, Protestantism). Those who rejected the restored faith were then given opportunities (multiple opportunities) to change their mind and recant their Protestant faith. As noted above, those who refused still had three choices: live quietly in England keeping their faith hidden; go into exile on the continent; or make their faith known and step forth as martyrs. An additional element contributing to this decision was finances. Exile to the continent was really only available to those with the means to support themselves there. Those with a fervent Protestant faith but insufficient funds to go into exile typically joined the prominent in becoming martyrs. For clergy, the choices were less clear, or perhaps more complex. Those who held Lutheran beliefs seem to have been allowed to continue as clergy, if they weren't married or if married had "put away" their wives. Those clergy who became martyrs were those Protestants who did not adhere to Lutheranism, would not turn their backs on their wives, or did not seek exile on the continent.

Ultimately, the Marian martyrs included several bishops (as noted earlier), along with a number of prominent priests, a number of laymen, including Thomas Drowry (a sixteen-year-old blind boy), and forty-eight laywomen. The chancellor of the Diocese of Gloucester who oversaw the trial of Drowry urged him to recant, saying, "Do as I have done." However, the boy refused, reminding the chancellor that he had learned his now-heretical beliefs from sermons the chancellor had given in the cathedral where the trial was being held, and he wasn't about to recant now.[4]

Those convicted of heresy also included such prominent clergy as John Rogers, who had completed the Tyndale Bible in The Netherlands after Tyndale's death (using the pseudonym Thomas Matthews). He was known for his fiery preaching and fervent Protestant faith, and he would be the first to be burned as a heretic in Mary's reign, dying at the stake in the Smithfield section of London on February 4, 1555. Many would follow, there and elsewhere. Perhaps the most notable burning occurred in Oxford, when Hugh Latimer, Nicholas Ridley, and Thomas Cranmer were tied together to the stake and burned. However, Cranmer's inclusion in this burning was not assured for some time, because he recanted and then refuted his recantation several times. When the time came for him to confirm his final recantation publicly, he refused. As the fire rose around him, he stretched out the hand with which he had signed the recantations, declaring that it had offended God, and therefore he wanted it to burn first.[5]

Many of those imprisoned and awaiting burning were cared for by a large group of elite women whose faith prompted them to stay in England (at least for a while) and turn their energies to supporting their imprisoned co-religionists. The generosity of these women included providing fruit, bread, and other foodstuffs, as well as letters of encouragement and new clean shirts, to these future martyrs. In these ways, some laywomen resisted the return

4. "The Reminiscences of John Louth," in Nichols, ed., *Narratives*, 78–80. Drowry had first appeared in court on March, 28, 1556.

5. MacCulloch, *Cranmer*, 603.

to Catholicism and continued to promote Protestantism. Meanwhile, the martyrs themselves, both lay and ordained, also resisted Catholicism in favor of Protestantism through their martyrdom as well as through their compassionate and encouraging pastoral care and letter-sermons. These activities were reciprocal: the women cared for the future martyrs and the future martyrs continued to promote Protestantism, writing sermons in the form of letters the women delivered to co-religionists. In these several ways the female caregivers—and those for whom they cared—further defined the role of the English laity in the English Reformation.[6]

Joan Wilkinson, who had served in Anne Boleyn's household and had received a shipment of Protestant books after the Queen's imprisonment, may have been one of the unofficial leaders of this group of women. She was often referred to by the honorific "Mother" Wilkinson, implying that she held a position of prominence and respect among both those who served and the martyrs who benefitted from these ministries. Some years later, after seeking exile in Frankfurt, she would write her will, declaring that she was a "voluntary exile for the true religion of Cryste."[7]

Hugh Latimer, former bishop of Worcester, voiced a common sentiment when he wrote to her, saying, "If the gift of a pot of cold water shall not be in oblivion with God, how can God forget your manifold and bountiful gifts, when he shall say unto you, 'I was in prison, and you visited me?'"[8]

Other women, working with Mrs. Wilkinson, included her cousin, Ann Warcup, and Mary Glover. Ann and her husband (Cuthbert) had a large house in Oxfordshire which served as a "Safe House" for prominent Protestants

6. Hooper, *Later Writings*, 602, 610; Bradford, *Writings*, 46.

7. PRO PROB 11/42B, fos. 233–35.

8. Hugh Latimer to Joan Wilkinson, ECL 260, fo. 276v.

travelling to the English Channel and ultimately the continent in search of exile. Joan Wilkinson and Anne Warcup often seem to have worked together in supporting the prisoners. Mary Glover had led a similar group of women in providing support to Bishop Latimer's string of preachers in the late-1530s. These women and many others cared for the Protestant martyrs in a variety of largely feminine ways. In addition to material support, like shirts and food, they also wrote letters of encouragement to many. They also wrote to at least one imprisoned laywoman, titling the letter with the words, "The letter of one faithful woman being at liberty to another in prison."

Most of the women who were involved in this ministry promoted their true religion (their religious identities) by employing the traditional feminine activities of providing food, clothing, health care, and nurture. In some cases, though, women from this group ignored the constraints of feminine norms to prepare and preach sermons to Protestants hungry for the Word and for guidance. Such was the case with Joyce Hailes, widow, and daughter-in-law of a prominent judge, who preached publicly in Coventry against a group of radical Protestants (the Freewillers), who went beyond the conventional Protestant theology of the day. They were the subject of several letters between Mrs. Hailes and the future martyrs and were also the target of sermon-letters written by the future martyrs that refuted all that this group espoused.[9]

These women, both Joyce Hailes and those employing more traditional means of encouragement, could effectively provide such support while simultaneously publicly proclaiming their religious beliefs and identities through their actions. The promotion of one's true religion had not offered such a dramatic opportunity to demonstrate

9. John Bradford to Joyce Hales, ECL MS 260, fos. 79–81v.

one's faith since the first centuries of Christianity. These activities enabled them to develop their religious identities more fully, as they simultaneously affiliated with their co-religionists and differentiated from those who supported Marian Catholicism. They moved between their internal and external selves in ways that allowed their actions also to influence and refine their beliefs. Some women, including Joan Wilkinson, appropriated established gender-coded behaviors for new purposes. Through their feminizing actions they redefined prisons as domestic spaces, performing within the prison setting feminine tasks normally relegated to the privacy of their households. But this action had a second consequence. The redefining of this space paradoxically also transformed these tasks from private domestic actions into public statements of resistance to official religious policy. These tasks thus became a quiet but potent vehicle for political as well as religious pronouncements while still remaining technically within the confines of the feminine. In these ways, they played an important role, as lay women, in shaping the Protestant Church that would re-emerge following the death of Mary and the accession to the throne of Elizabeth.

While many Protestants willingly put themselves forward as martyrs, not all did. Among those who served as caregivers, many received advice urging them to follow Jesus's example of going into exile, as he did when he went into Samaria on his way from Judea back to Galilee. For instance, future martyrs urged Joan Wilkinson and Anne Warcup to seek exile in one of the Protestant cities on the continent. In writing to Mrs. Wilkinson, Cranmer exhorted her: "withdraw yourself from the malice of your & God's enemies, into some place where God is most purely served, . . . preserving of yourself to God . . . & to the society & comfort of Christ's little flock." Ultimately, Mrs. Wilkinson, along with Cuthbert and Anne Warcup, and Anne Hooper, wife of John Hooper, and their son sought exile in Frankfurt in 1555.[10] They were joined by many others who had the funds to leave England and live in exile in protestant cities on the continent, including Geneva, Strasbourg, Emden, Zurich, and Frankfurt. Most of these exiles were either priests or merchants or had close relationships with such folk, giving them the means to support themselves while living in exile.

One group of English exiles had arrived in Frankfurt in June 1554 and soon found themselves immersed in what became known as "The Troubles at Frankfurt." This was a struggle among English exiles from across continental Europe concerning the style of worship to be followed by the Frankfurt exiles' worship community. Ultimately, these "Troubles" previewed the struggles that would develop between the established Church and Calvinists in England during the reign of Elizabeth I and beyond. They also reveal yet another way the continental reformations influenced the religion of the English during the Reformation there. Additionally, they illustrate one of the ways the laity was involved in this Reformation. As members of the congregation they voted, along with the clergy, on matters of religious policy that defined their worshipping community.

With the magistrates' approval, the newly arrived exiles soon arranged to share a church with French Protestant exiles who had fled France and then England, each having a time for worship in their own language. Subsequently, they decided to use the second *Prayer Book* from Edward VI's reign (with some substantial modifications, most notably eliminating audible responses from the congregation) as the

---

10. John Hooper to Joan Wilkinson, in Foxe, *Book of Martyrs*, Book 11 (1570, p. 1691); Thomas Cranmer to Joan Wilkinson, ECL MS 262, fo. 214v.

basis for their worship. Since, according to one of the exiles, they were the first group of English exiles to organize themselves for worship and have a place to gather, they wrote to several groups who had gone to other cities in the German States, the Netherlands, and Switzerland to invite them to come to Frankfurt. The recipients of these letters seem to have misinterpreted their content and responded with suggestions as to who should take charge of the Frankfurt worshipping community. In any case, these first exiles in Frankfurt were soon joined by people from the other exile communities on the continent, including Richard Chambers, a wealthy layman, and the Rev. Edmund Grindal, the future archbishop of Canterbury, both of whom came from Strasbourg.

John Knox, who had been impatient with the pace of reform in England during Edward's reign and who had sought exile in Calvin's Geneva, decided to go to Frankfurt in September 1554 to get that community of exiles moving toward "right" (read: Calvinist) religion. Hearing that they were using a version of the second *Prayer Book* as the basis for their worship would have been a "red flag" for him. He had opposed many things in that *Prayer Book* when it was introduced in England, and he was determined to make sure none of the exiles took such a step backwards, away from true reform. His arrival triggered what became known as, "The Troubles at Frankfurt," as debate broke out concerning the form of worship to be used there.

As noted earlier, the congregation had been using a heavily edited version of the second *Book of Common Prayer*, in their services. However, as people arrived and joined this vital community, there seems to have been a decrease in the enthusiasm for this order. The men from Strasburg commandeered the worship space and led worship using the unedited *Book of Common Prayer*, including exuberant responses from the congregation, leading to outrage from other members of the community. Meanwhile, at least two new books of worship were developed by selected members of the congregation. Additionally, Knox and several others brought with them copies of the *Order of Geneva*, the book used by Calvinist congregations in Europe. The Orders of Worship developed within the Frankfurt community were based substantially on this book. However, the congregation did not adopt any of these proposed Orders. Rather, they continued to use the edited *Prayer Book*.

Then, several new exiles, including the future bishop of Ely, the Rev. Richard Cox, arrived in March 1555. They were not pleased with using either the edited *Book of Common Prayer* or any of the more Calvinist alternatives. Ultimately, they prevailed, John Knox returned to Geneva, and the full second *Prayer Book* of Edward VI became the standard for worship in the community. This may have ended the struggles in Frankfurt; however, such struggles over forms of worship between the Calvinists and those who preferred the *Prayer Book* would continue in England through the reign of Elizabeth I and beyond. In fact, contention over forms of worship rather than beliefs within the English Church is not surprising, given that Thomas Cranmer and the other leaders of the Church under Edward VI had created a Church defined by its liturgy rather than its doctrine.

Meanwhile, as the exiles settled into their chosen communities on the continent, they did not forget those co-religionists who had chosen to stay in England. They were involved in a vigorous book trade in Protestant books written in English, and mostly printed in Antwerp. The beneficiaries of these books were those who had remained in England during Mary's reign.

MARY'S MARRIAGE TO PHILIP OF SPAIN

As religion in the realm began to change back to some form of Catholicism, efforts were underway to find a suitable husband for Mary, and she seems to have given Charles V (her cousin) full responsibility for making the choice. He, in turn, had urged his son, Philip, to disentangle himself from some similar negotiations with Portugal so that he would be available. Philip's chief competitor for Mary's hand was the Englishman Edward Courtenay, son of one of her oldest supporters. He was favored by many within Mary's Privy Council and her chamber. However, Mary doesn't seem to have ever seriously considered Courtenay. By the beginning of September 1553, the real issue was not whom Mary would marry, but whether she would marry Philip or not. She was ready, having already confessed to being "half in love" with him after seeing his picture. Convincing the Council and the people would be harder, much harder. On November 16, she rejected a petition from the Commons that she marry within the realm, much to the consternation of her subjects. In the end, Mary and Philip were married in July 1554, despite pleas from the Privy Councilors and Parliament that she not marry him. This marriage was one of Mary's biggest mistakes.

Philip was styled as king jointly with Mary as queen, but with no rights of survivorship if Mary died childless (as she did, after an apparent pregnancy turned out to be "false"). However, that did not assuage the people. The fear was that England would become a Spanish pawn, a very real possibility. The English people at all levels distrusted the Spanish. Four simultaneous rebellions were planned for 1554, although none ever got off the ground. However, English suspicion of Philip was justified, as he did seize control of foreign policy. Two years later, Philip became king of Spain and within a year he had dragged England into war with France. If the "Spanish match" was one of Mary's worst mistakes, some aspects of her religious policy (as it developed) were her other, and Philip's influence was evident here too.

PROGRESS IN THE RESTORATION OF CATHOLICISM

The restoration of Catholicism had begun with the return of traditional liturgy and other pious practices to the churches of England. Catholic images were returned to church interiors and were valued for the inspiration they brought to the worshippers. Religious policy promoted Catholic worship and focused on the need to revitalize the priests and bishops, with respect to discipline, loyalty to Rome, and education. Cardinal Pole felt this revitalization was necessary before it would be feasible to introduce inspired preaching, a key part of the European Catholic Reformation (which had begun in 1545 in the Council of Trent and would continue beyond the end of Mary's reign). Further, without adequate discipline and education there was always the danger that such inspiration might lead to utterances from the pulpit that would cause some to leave the Church. To improve preaching, Bishop Edward Bonner of London published his own *Book of Homilies* in 1555. This volume may have helped improve the sermons parishioners heard, but there is no clear evidence of how widely it was used. Meanwhile, the Crown, including both Mary and Philip as well as Cardinal Pole, also defined the boundaries between the religion of this reign and that of the previous time, motivated as they were by a desire to achieve doctrinal conformity and eliminate heresy (i.e., Protestantism). As noted earlier, they enforced these boundaries by imprisoning prominent Protestants, both laity and clergy.

While leaders of Protestantism from the previous reign had either fled to the continent or were being executed as heretics, through the first four years of Mary's reign a preponderance of the laity were seeing their spiritual health nurtured in welcome ways. They appreciated the familiar sights, smells, and cadence of the Mass. They welcomed the return to their traditional faith and pious practices. In fact, the statistical sample taken from wills written in the Diocese of Gloucester during this time shows a marked increase in the number of traditional will preambles during Mary's reign. This sample also reveals changes in the content of such preambles, with testators including more detail than in Henry's reign, to elaborate on or explain their traditional beliefs, and give more attention to Christ's passion and death.[11] For instance, Joan Holder, a Gloucestershire widow, bequeathed her soul

> To Almighty God my creator and redeemer unto whose mercy I commit my self unto [sic], trusting by the merits of his passion to inherit the kingdom of heaven, and also desiring our blessed Lady with all the whole company of heaven to pray for me.[12]

A year later, John Dyston committed his soul

> To Almighty God and to Jesus Christ his only son and to all the holy blessed company of heaven most steadfastly believing that the thing that is committed to their charge cannot perish but be preserved and in better wise be restored at the latter day.[13]

11. Litzenberger, *The English Reformation and the Laity,* 91–94.

12. GRO, Gloucestershire Wills 1556/64.

13. GRO, Gloucestershire Wills 1557/224.

Both of these testators embraced traditional religion and welcomed the Marian restoration of Catholicism but gave greater emphasis than had their traditional predecessors to Jesus Christ and his suffering and death on the cross as they elaborated on their basic faith in their wills. Additionally, while wills are often viewed as lagging indicators of whatever truths they reveal because they are typically written by the elderly, that was arguably not the case during Mary's reign. In 1557–58 all of Europe was engulfed in an influenza epidemic that killed more people than any illness since the Black Death. Young and old succumbed, and young, as well as old, left wills bequeathing their souls in ways inspired by their mostly traditional faith.[14]

MARIAN CATHOLICISM'S CHALLENGES TO CONFORMING PARISHES

Mary's restoration of Catholicism to England focused in the first instance on restoring worship and the spaces within which it occurred. Restoring parish choirs may not have required funding beyond hiring an organist/choir director; however, other restorations would require significant funds. For instance, where communion tables had replaced altars, the churchwardens needed to retrieve the altars from their hiding places (often in someone's barn), or if that wasn't possible, pay to have a new altar constructed. Similarly, the rood loft needed to be restored. If the statues had merely been hidden during Edward's reign, they could be retrieved. However, if they had been destroyed, the churchwardens had to have a sculptor or woodworker create them anew. That would require time as well as money, so churches that

14. Marcombe, *English Small Town Life*, 227.

were anxious to conform, like St. Michael's in Gloucester, also paid to have the images that typically appeared on the rood loft (the crucifix, Mary, and John), painted on an oil cloth that could be temporarily hung on the reconstructed rood loft until the actual statues were completed. The cost of less significant individual items still added up. At St. Michael's the churchwardens purchased liturgical books, bought back vestments and stoles (purchased a few years earlier by parishioners), and purchased fabric for new albs for a total cost of £6, a significant sum in 1554.[15]

A PREMATURE END TO THE RESTORATION

In September 1558, St. Michael's paid to have the completed crucifix and the statues of Mary and John mounted on their rood loft. Two months later, Mary died, probably of influenza. She had not had a child, and Philip (by statute) could not succeed her. Therefore, she was followed on the throne by Elizabeth I, her Protestant half-sister and the daughter of Henry VIII and Anne Boleyn. St. Michael's rood loft with its statues would come down a short time later. Mary's approach to restoring Catholicism to her realm had been sound, despite the complications of her marriage to Philip, but she ran out of time.[16] The religion that followed in England took some time to achieve clarity for the monarch's subjects, but Elizabeth would reign for forty-three years, so there would be time, as there hadn't been during Edward's short reign, to become accustomed to Protestantism.

15. GRO P154/14 CW 1/7.
16. GRO P154/14 CW 1/1, 1/11.

DISCUSSION QUESTIONS

1. Was it a political mistake for the leaders of England in Mary's reign to burn so many people as heretics? Why?

2. Why do you think most English people welcomed the restoration of Catholicism?

3. Most historians have judged Mary's reign to have been a failure. Do you agree or disagree with this judgment? Why?

4. How do you think English religion would have been different if Mary had lived another twenty years? Why?

5

ELIZABETHAN RELIGION, IN ALL ITS DIVERSITY

(1558–1603)

WHAT WERE THE PEOPLE thinking? Many of them had been alive during Henry VIII's last years. They had lived through the English Catholicism of those years, the powerful Protestantism of Edward's reign, and the restoration of Catholicism, so abruptly ended by Mary's sudden death. Edward's reign had lasted just six and a half years, Mary's just five and a half! Not long enough for either Protestantism or Catholicism to take hold. The dizzying speed and dramatic difference between these religious policies must have left people, both lay and clergy, apprehensive about what was to come. Additionally, by the time of Elizabeth, people may have become less inclined to follow the monarch's religion blindly—to see the health of their souls as linked inextricably to the monarch's religion. The pendulum swings had taken their toll. Exposure to multiple sets of beliefs and practices (without apparent harm to one's soul) had opened people to a range of religious possibilities. There was still some sense of there being just one true religion. However, there were numerous possibilities of what that religion should be.

During Edward's reign, the official religion was Protestantism, while most of the people clung to the Catholicism with which they had been raised. (Lawrence Humphrey, who would emerge as a leader of a protest over vestments in the mid-1560s and later as dean of Gloucester, lamented the lack of commitment by the people, which he saw as a key factor in the failure of Edwardian Protestantism to be more solidly established before Edward's death.) Then during Mary's reign, a form of Catholicism replaced Protestantism as the official religion of the land, and most of the people seem to have been overjoyed that they could continue to practice the religion of their childhood. However, a critical group of people had embraced the new religion under Edward and resisted all efforts to persuade them to reject it. The fact that the Queen was Catholic was not sufficiently persuasive.

With the accession of Elizabeth I to the throne on November 17, 1558, people's religious choices expanded. On the one hand, there were the Catholics whose allegiance to the traditional faith would threaten to imperil them and lead to some creative ways of obscuring and expressing their faith simultaneously. On the other, there were the followers of Calvinism who were much more likely to manifest their faith stridently and publicly in order to draw attention to the perceived errors of Elizabethan Protestantism and draw others to their beliefs and practices. The English Church, as it had been structured under Edward and continued under

Elizabeth, still had bishops playing a key role in the authoritative hierarchy, and many of the *Prayer Book* prayers were either direct translations or only slightly altered prayers from the Mass. These characteristics led to the charge that the English Church was but half-reformed at the time of Elizabeth's accession. However, this was the Church and the *Prayer Book* with which many parishioners had just begun to become familiar when Edward died. Some of these folks had died for their faith, while others had gone into exile or hidden in place in England during Mary's reign. Additionally, while the boundary between Catholicism and Elizabethan Protestantism became increasingly clear, that was not the case for the boundary between the Calvinists and the Queen's religion. The latter boundary was blurred, by both effective proselytizing and the lack of clarity as to what constituted Elizabethan Protestantism. Elizabeth's reign would be characterized by her desire to define English Protestantism as broadly as possible. However, not even that was initially discernible.

This chapter will continue to add layers to the understanding of the influence of other Reformations on that in England. It will also continue to explore the role of the laity in the process and policies of religious change in England during this period and contribute further to our understanding of the origins of the Church of England and all Anglican and Episcopal churches of the twenty-first century.

THE FIRST DECADE OF ELIZABETH'S REIGN

Initially, Elizabethan Protestantism restored many of the beliefs and practices of the last years of Edward VI's reign, combined with some moderating influences from the earlier years of that reign. Once again, changes in religious policy focused on changing the liturgy. Thus, the churchwardens of St. Michael's, Gloucester paid to have the dirt removed, once again, from beneath the altar and chancel area of their church. The return of some form of Protestantism may have reassured some people, but exactly what did that religion include? The Royal Articles and Injunctions of 1559, on the one hand, and the new *Prayer Book* from that same year, on the other, give an initial answer to this question, albeit a somewhat conflicted one. The new *Prayer Book* opted in several cases for the more traditional provisions of the book from 1549, the first *Prayer Book*. Most crucially, it included the provision that clergy wear the vestments they had worn in the second year of Edward VI's reign. That earlier book had specified that priests were to wear cassock and surplice when presiding at Morning and Evening Prayer, and an alb, with either a chasuble or a cope when presiding at Holy Communion. However, the reforming of the Christian religion had continued over the ten years that had elapsed since that earlier book. John Calvin was now leading Swiss Reform, and numerous English clergy liked the latest changes they had experienced while living in exile in cities such as Zurich and Geneva while Mary was on the throne in England. They believed that it was more scripturally sound to wear a Geneva gown (a loose large-sleeved black academic gown) when presiding at worship services than to wear elaborate eye-catching garb that might distract from the centrality of the Word of God. This difference would lead to resistance from some later in the 1560s.[1]

Meanwhile, the conflict between the Visitation Articles and Injunctions, on the one hand, and the *Book of Common Prayer*, on the other, was most notable with regard to the nature of Communion bread. The Injunctions

1. *Prayer Book, 1559*, 41.

specified that "wafer-bread" was to be used, while the *Prayer Book* called for bread that "is usual to be eaten at table,"[2] that is, loaf bread. Concern regarding this difference was felt immediately in some areas but would continue as an issue through the first half of Elizabeth's reign. Some bishops wanted to enforce consistency regarding the bread and were frustrated by the lack of clarity from the top as to what that uniformity would look like. Some asked the archbishop of Canterbury, Matthew Parker, for guidance. Parker's advice, in at least one case, was: "for the sake of peace and quietness here and there, to be content" with the use of either wafers or ordinary bread at Communion.[3] This ambiguity led to contention among parishioners in some dioceses. Additionally, it contributed to the lack of clarity and to the unease of many English people who were anxious to know definitively what their religion was to be. They knew that the monarch was supposed to determine this, but so far, she had not done so with sufficient clarity in their eyes. She had been far too vague.

Yet, the people knew that the *Prayer Book* and Royal Injunctions would not be the only factors in determining official religious policy. There was also the question of the queen's marriage. Certainly, she would marry. Her sister had. All women, at least all women with social standing, did. All monarchs did! After all, one of the primary duties of a monarch was to produce an heir. And whom Elizabeth would marry could definitely influence the future religious policy of England. Wouldn't the queen's husband determine her (and the realm's) religion? That is in all likelihood what the people, at all social levels, expected. So, who were

2. Hughes and Larkin, eds., *Tudor Royal Proclamations*, vol. II, 131; *Prayer Book, 1559*, 106.

3. Parkhurst, *Letter Book*, 243, 247; Wark, *Elizabethan Recusancy in Cheshire*, 18n.

Queen Elizabeth's potential suitors? There were certainly plenty of possibilities, including her former brother-in-law, now King Phillip II of Spain. However, the most serious candidates were Robert Dudley, her childhood friend and the Earl of Leicester (a Protestant), and a number of foreign aspirants, including the king of Denmark (a Protestant), and the French dauphin (or prince and heir to the French throne, a Catholic).

However, even ten years on, Elizabeth had not chosen a husband. So that particular potential influence on religious policy remained unknown, as it would for the rest of her reign. Elizabeth used the possibility of her marriage to control her closest advisors on numerous occasions. Meanwhile, the myth of the "virgin queen" emerged in East Anglia at the end of that first decade as a popular argument against the possibility that the queen might marry the French prince. The people, at least in East Anglia, seem to have preferred that she not marry if French dominance was the alternative.

In summary, ambiguity was the watchword of the first decade of Elizabeth's reign, although both Catholics and Calvinists in England were hopeful of further change in their direction. The Catholics were expecting the pope to excommunicate the queen which would negate her sacred anointing and free them to revolt and replace her on the throne with someone of their own choosing. Meanwhile, the Calvinists saw their chance for further reform in the convocation of clergy to be held at St. Paul's Cathedral in 1563. The convocation came sooner than the pope's excommunication of Elizabeth.

NEXT STEPS IN CREATING
ELIZABETHAN PROTESTANTISM

On 11 January 1563, nearly five years into the new reign, Archbishop Matthew Parker mounted the broad steps that led from his barge, moored at a dock on the Thames, to St. Paul's Cathedral in the City of London where the Elizabethan clergy were assembled. These clergy harbored various levels of hope and anxiety concerning the religion of the realm, as official religious policy remained vague. In attendance were clergy who aligned with one of three groups: those who had remained active in the Marian (Catholic) Church and were hoping against hope for a return to some form of Catholicism; bishops, priests, and deacons, who had remained quietly in England during Mary's reign and hoped that the outcome of this gathering would define the *status quo* more clearly; and the Calvinists, labelled by some as "precisians" and comprised primarily of former Marian exiles, who were hoping for more reform, such as many had witnessed in Switzerland.

Those who preferred to keep things as they were, and particularly the bishops in this group, dominated the proceedings. Their goal was to clarify current Elizabethan religious policy, not to change it. A set of Thirty-Nine Articles of Religion, based on a similar set of forty-two articles drafted at the end of Edward VI's reign, occupied a large portion of the time and energy of the convocation. A number of these articles affirmed conventional Protestant doctrine. Other articles rejected the Catholic eucharistic doctrine of transubstantiation and radical Protestant beliefs, such as adult or believer's baptism (which was in the reality of the time, *re*baptism). These articles were approved, as were a very conventional *Catechism* prepared by Alexander Nowell, the dean of St. Paul's Cathedral, and a second *Book of Homilies*, which affirmed and expanded upon current religious policy.

However, a set of proposals submitted by Bishop Edwin Sandys, who was counted among the more radical Protestants, and two other sets proposed by a group of similarly minded clergy, were not approved. All would have modified the liturgy stipulated in the *Prayer Book* to move it in a more reformed direction. Sandys's proposals included eliminating both private baptism and the making of the sign of the cross on infants during their baptism. (Both had been abolished by the second *Book of Common Prayer* but had returned in the *Book* of 1559.) A third proposal would have established a committee to draft canons with which to govern the Church in England. (The English Church was still using the modified set of the canons of the Catholic Church introduced during Henry's reign.) The proposals from parish priests focused on simplifying worship further, another way to continue reforming the English Church. None of these were approved. The proposals submitted by the parish priests were not even considered by the bishops.[4]

The Calvinists had high hopes for the convocation of 1563, but alas, their hopes had been dashed. The possibilities of further reform were looking very bleak. However, these clergy were not ready to give up, so they turned their attention to clergy vestments. Fundamentally, they believed that the elaborate vestments of Elizabethan worship distracted in dangerous ways from the Word—from proclaiming the Scriptures, both the reading of biblical passages and the edifying preaching inspired by these passages. They also believed that distinctive street garb, such as the square cap, marked clergy out unnecessarily, and hindered their primary calling as clergy. Nothing but nothing was to get in the way of the peoples' access to the Scriptures which were

4. Stryp, *Annals*, vol. 1, part 1, 471–87, 499–516, 525–27.

after all the sole source of authority for these Christians. The clergy were to be essentially invisible conduits of the Word.

This belief in the perniciousness of vestments had been espoused some fifteen years earlier, in the reign of Edward VI during the most radical official Protestantism ever experienced in England. It was then that John Hooper was imprisoned for several months when he refused to don the required vestments for his ordination as bishop of Gloucester. His imprisonment ended only when he agreed to a compromise. He would vest appropriately for his ordination, which took place in London, but would never be required to wear those garments in his diocese.

Stripping away elaborate vestments—like albs, chasubles, and even surplices—was definitely not the position of the queen or the Church leaders. So, when some clergy chose to lead worship wearing only a Geneva gown, they attracted the attention of the Church leadership. This disobedience appeared in various places in England where there were Calvinist clergy or students. Members of St. John's College, Cambridge protested by burning their surplices (required vestments for college chapel worship). Some clergy in London, including, most notably, Robert Crowley of St. Giles-without-Cripplegate, didn't think that surplices (even when worn by choristers) were appropriate for worship services of any kind. Crowley became increasingly defiant, even preaching without a license on more than one occasion. Outside London, too, some clergy defied the requirements concerning vestments. This was the case of the Rev. Lawrence Humphries, president of Magdalen College at Oxford, and the archdeacon of Coventry, Thomas Lever.

However, the issue of elaborate vestments extended beyond the ordained and even beyond choir members and college students. Parishioners also stepped into the fray, on both sides. In Shrewsbury, a priest smiled approvingly when the rector preached against vestments. Some parishioners noticed this, and a fight ensued between pro- and anti-vestment laymen. Sometime later, that same minister wore a surplice when he preached, which led to his being attacked by a group of women. They threw stones at him, then pulled him out of the pulpit and tore his surplice![5] St. Giles and The Rev. Crowley continued to be at the center of the dispute. Eventually Crowley resigned from St. Giles and was relieved of all his other positions. However, these actions did not silence him. Rather, he turned to publishing pamphlets, beginning with one titled, *A Briefe Discourse against the Outward Apparel and Ministering Garments of the Popishe Church*, identified by the great Reformation historian Patrick Collinson as "the earliest Puritan manifesto."[6]

CATHOLIC RESISTANCE

Returning momentarily to the first decade of Elizabeth's reign, English Catholics had been waiting impatiently for either Elizabeth's marriage or the pope's excommunication of her to open the door to the return of Catholicism. The latter action would have negated her anointing with holy oil as a representative of God in her role as monarch. In turn, followers of the old religion in England would have been released from their allegiance to the queen and freed to defy her authority without fear of either treason or eternal damnation (for having overthrown an anointed monarch).

Meanwhile, Mary Stuart, queen of Scots, a Catholic and Elizabeth's cousin, had arrived in England. Mary had been born a week before her father, King James V of

5. Stowe, "Historical Memoranda of John Stowe: General, 1564–7" in Stowe, *Three Fifteen-Century Chronicles*, 128–47.

6. Collinson, *Puritan Movement*, 77.

Scotland, had died. She would eventually rule Scotland in her own right. However, her reign was a constant source of drama and scandal. This eventually led to her imprisonment in Leven Castle in Scotland from which she escaped in 1568. She then fled to England where the drama continued. She became involved in a series of plots to overthrow Elizabeth and place her, Mary Stuart, on the English throne.

When, by 1569, the queen still hadn't married and the pope still hadn't acted, a group of northern nobles hoping for a return to Catholicism lost patience and mounted a revolt to overthrow the queen and replace her on the throne with Mary Stuart. This revolt was quickly put down, and the related conspiracy, was revealed. This plot, known as the Ridolphi Plot, was just one of the conspiracies to which the former Scottish queen lent her support. It called for Elizabeth's excommunication to come first and be followed by the revolt in northern England. Perhaps the revolt would have attracted more supporters and have succeeded if the queen had previously been excommunicated. Two years later, in 1571, the pope did excommunicate Elizabeth, but it was too late. As for Mary, queen of Scots, after some years under house arrest and her involvement in more plots, pressure mounted for her execution. However, Elizabeth was very reluctant to authorize the execution of her cousin, a previously anointed monarch. Ultimately though, her Privy Council prevailed, and Mary was executed. Yet, these actions did not eliminate Elizabethan Catholicism.

Official religious policy did become clearer as the second decade of Elizabeth's reign began, but adherents of the traditional religion still found ways to stay true to their religion. There seem to have been two options available to them: become a recusant (one who refused to attend Sunday services) or become a church papist (one whose actions gave the impression of full participation in the life and worship of their parish, while carefully avoiding taking Communion and striving to ignore the teachings of Elizabethan Protestantism). The authorities in Rome definitely preferred the first option through most of Elizabeth's reign. They felt that anything less than full absence from worship could imperil the souls of their faithful followers. However, the English recusancy laws were primarily targeted against those Catholics who refused to attend their parish church, and the penalty was significant: at least substantial fines, and frequently loss of property and even imprisonment with the possibility of death. Thus, the costs of adhering to Rome's guidance were very high.

Yet, there was a third option of sorts. Some husbands of recusant wives, those with sufficient means, might seek exile on the continent, as did John Pauncefoot, lord of the manor of Hasfield in Gloucester. He and his son fled to Douai in 1584, the home of a seminary preparing priests for missionary work in Elizabethan England. Pauncefoot's wife, Dorothy, was imprisoned for her recusancy at the same time as her husband and their son went into exile. However, she did not remain in prison for long. After her release, she continued to absent herself from worship services at St. Mary's Church in Hasfield and took advantage of her freedom to minister to Catholic priests and laypeople, imprisoned for their faith. In this way, she followed in the footsteps of the numerous Protestant women who had ministered to the imprisoned future Protestant martyrs of Mary's reign some two decades earlier.

Meanwhile, fines or imprisonment, indeed, loomed over men and some women accused of recusancy. This happened all over England during Elizabeth's reign. A case in point was Margaret Clitheroe. Born and raised a Protestant, she converted to Catholicism, curiously, after marrying a Protestant. She manifested her faith by supporting and hiding Catholic priests and by providing the sacramental vessels needed for celebrations of the Mass. She was imprisoned and released several times, but once the authorities found those vessels, she was imprisoned once again, and this time, executed as a Catholic martyr.[7]

Additionally, in many cases, married women were accused, but it was their husbands who paid the price. The imprisonment and other punishments of Catholics in Elizabethan England increased after Parliament passed a new law in 1581 that, among other things, declared that Catholics were committing treason by pledging allegiance to the pope, a foreign ruler. Also, both that law and the statute of 1593 changed the possibility of punishing wives directly. However, despite the specific law in place at the time, the government did find ways to punish women. Some, like Margaret Clitheroe, even died as a result, as did many men, and most of the apprehended priests.

As implied earlier, priests did have ways to hide from the authorities, most frequently thanks to the hospitality of women with large houses. These women and their husbands had their houses modified to create "priest holes," secret places (often next to a fireplace), where priests could hide if the authorities came around. Most were in country estates with otherwise comfortable accommodations for the visiting priests, who celebrated Mass regularly while in residence.

The other option for Elizabethan Catholics, church papistry, brought much milder penalties. Elizabeth wanted people to attend worship in their parish church but was not concerned with what they believed in private. Church Papists went to church, sometimes even serving in leadership

7. Verner, "Catholic Communities," 89; *History of the County of Gloucester,* vol. 8, 2282–90; Hickerson, "In Control of Conscience," 81–86.

positions in their congregation. However, they did their best to protect themselves from pernicious (that is, Protestant) beliefs and worship. They did this by occupying themselves with praying the rosary or silently reciting other Catholic prayers during worship, by sitting as far from the pulpit as possible, so they wouldn't be able to hear the preacher, or at least, by claiming to be "out of charity with their neighbor" and therefore not qualified to receive Communion. The milder treatment of church papists, as opposed to the harsher treatment of recusants, illustrates Elizabeth's desire to regulate actions rather than beliefs. This approach, in turn, contributed substantially to the creation of a diverse Elizabethan Church, a Church marked by diversity within unity. Yes, limits were enforced on unacceptable actions but not on beliefs held quietly by individuals, another way sixteenth-century actions and policies helped create the Church we know today.

Throughout Elizabeth's reign, Catholics continued to strive to stay true to their religion. Meanwhile, the Spanish and the pope had not given up on the possibility of turning England back into a Catholic country. King Philip of Spain amassed an armada for this purpose, which sailed toward England with the pope's blessing in 1577. Along the way, they stopped to take on board troops who would land in England after the defeat of the English navy. Unfortunately, the troops were delayed. The Spanish ships were well built and sailed in an impenetrable crescent-shaped flotilla. However, these facts would not help them as they sat at anchor waiting for those troops. While they waited, the English loaded some old ships with flammable material, set them on fire, and set them adrift so that they would float into the midst of the Armada. To avoid these ships, the Spanish ships cut their anchor lines and sailed north in the Channel. Unfortunately for the Spanish, the wind then came up and blew the Armada off course. Without their anchors, they could not re-group and could only sail on north and around the northern coasts of Scotland and Ireland, suffering colossal losses along the way. Meanwhile, in England, the strong wind was seen as a "Protestant Wind," sent by God to affirm and protect Elizabethan England from the threat of the Spanish Armada. Catholicism would not vanish from the realm, but efforts by foreign powers to eliminate Protestantism did come to an end with the Armada.

RADICAL PROTESTANT CHALLENGES

Catholics threatened the established religion through non-participation and nonpayment of tithes, and threatened the Crown with sedition, given their allegiance to the pope. The radical Protestants (or Calvinists, as they sometimes called themselves), on the other hand, wanted to change Elizabethan Protestantism, not turn their backs on it. Beginning in the very first decade of Elizabeth's reign with the controversy over vestments, resistance to official religious policy and attempts to change official religious policy came mostly from this group, and their efforts continued throughout the reign. The story of their labors reveals additional ways in which both the English laity and continental reformations (especially Calvinist reform), influenced religious change during this phase of the English Reformation.

In 1571, Lawrence Chaderton, member of Parliament from Cambridge, stood on the floor of the House of Commons and advocated for a Church without bishops, essentially Presbyterianism. The discussion that followed led the queen to decree that religious policy not be discussed in Parliament. One Peter Wentworth took issue with this restriction and was imprisoned for a time for his efforts.

Meanwhile, those with Presbyterian sympathies might have been silenced, but they would not vanish from England.

Meanwhile, in the Diocese of Gloucester in the 1570s, Bishop Cheyney contended with Protestants who stayed away from church (sometimes known as "separating Protestants" but whom he called "Puritans") and he was anxious to punish them. He may have received the same message from the queen as had Bishops Aylmer (of London) and Freke (of Norwich), to focus equally on punishing radical Protestants and Catholics, but he tended to ignore the Catholics.[8] Numerous Protestants were brought before the Church courts in his diocese during that time. Their reasons for staying away from church seemed to focus on the priest's wearing a surplice (as was required by the Ornaments Rubric in the *Prayer Book* of 1559), his failure to use loaf-bread for communion (as stipulated in the Injunctions of 1559 but not in the *Prayer Book,* which called for wafers), and his insistence on using the font for baptisms.

One case regarding baptism was particularly fraught. William Drewett and his wife, of St. Nicholas in Gloucester, persistently refused to have their baby baptized, because the priest insisted on using the parish font, rather than a nearby stream, pond, or lake, or even the River Severn. The Church court ordered officers of the court to go to the Drewett's house, seize the baby, and bring it to the parish church on the following Sunday to be baptized. They could not accomplish this, so the parents were ordered to appear in court again. There, they affirmed that their baby had not been baptized. They said they did not respect the Church of England as the Church of Christ, and they would not consent to having their child baptized. If it were taken from them by force and baptized in the font, they would never

8. Bishop Cheyney to the Privy Council, 24 October 1577 PRO/ SP 12/117/12.

take it back or consider it to be their child—ever! However, this was not the end of the story.

Two weeks later, Drewett and his wife once again appeared in court. This time, he was holding their baby. After he refused to hand the baby to the midwife who was present, the midwife was ordered to take it from him, but she was not able to do so. Both Drewett and his wife were then sent to prison—separate prisons. He was directed to give the baby to his wife, so she could nurse it. He refused and took it to prison with him, where it would have no access to any sustenance. He felt that strongly about the baby not being baptized in a font and was worried that his wife wasn't strong enough to keep the baby from being taken from her. Fortunately, both Drewett and his wife were released from prison before their baby starved. However, William Drewett was imprisoned once again, this time in Newgate Prison in London, where another Gloucester father of an unbaptized infant was also imprisoned.[9]

In addition to refusing to have their children baptized in the parish font, many of the more radical Protestants also sometimes went "gadding" to hear "lively" sermons in neighboring parishes on Sunday afternoons, after attending their parish churches in the morning. These sermons were theologically more aligned with their own beliefs. However, attending them was a technical violation of the law, which required that lay people attend their parish church and *only* their parish church. Additionally, they took notes during sermons and might meet with friends, even fellow parishioners, in a conventicle (a private, illegal religious gathering where they might discuss their sermon notes, pray, study the Scriptures, or worship without the *Prayer Book*). For many Calvinists (who by the later 1570s were generally

9. GRO, Gloucester Diocesan Records, vol. XXXV, 65, 110–11, 114, 116–17.

being labeled as "Puritans), these activities were welcome alternatives to ordinary parish worship. In these gatherings, they could pray extemporaneously, which they considered much more edifying that reading prayers from a book, even the *Book of Common Prayer*. In any case, they usually continued to attend their parish church.

Another challenge to official policy came from participation in the exercises or prophesyings, initially offered in Swiss cities to provide continuing scriptural education for ordained ministers but sometimes including laymen, as well. These had initially been introduced in England in the early 1550s by Bishop Hooper in Gloucester. They were reintroduced early in Elizabeth's reign by clergy who had lived in exile during Mary's reign. They became an issue of concern, because they often involved laymen, as well as clergy, and perhaps more significantly, because they culminated in sermons, often preached by clergy without licenses to do so. Edmund Grindal became archbishop of Canterbury in 1576 and soon was embroiled in a dispute with the Crown over the continuation of these exercises, which he supported. As a result, he was sidelined as archbishop, imprisoned, and prohibited from carrying out the normal responsibilities of his office. The exercises were declared illegal and shut down.

In 1583, John Whitgift replaced Edmund Grindal as archbishop of Canterbury and launched a concerted effort to eliminate the presbyterian movement and dismantle the policies that had encouraged radical Protestantism under Grindal. However, it soon became clear that those promoting a presbyterian form of church polity (with no bishops) were not going away. Three years after Whitgift's elevation, a series of pamphlets, known as the Marprelate Tracts, began to appear. These tracts were written anonymously and printed secretly between October 1588 and September

1589. They were marked by irony and insult and seemed to attack specific bishops. They shocked their readers. Their aim was to discredit bishops and the polity of the Elizabethan Church that gave these men regional authority over the Church. However, they would not succeed in changing the Church during Elizabeth's reign or those of her immediate successors.[10]

All in all, though, Calvinist efforts to change Elizabethan Protestantism were not easily suppressed, and in fact, did result in changes to the established Church, although bishops continued to have authority over their dioceses. Interestingly, these changes did not arise from their key objections, regarding vestments, Communion bread, or baptism. Rather, they focused on making the worship space more hospitable to the Word of God, mainly by whitewashing the walls and providing a well-placed lectern and pulpit for proclaiming God's Word. By the end of Elizabeth's reign, the Calvinists had largely accomplished this goal. Once again, the focus was on worship and the spaces where it happened.

THE SHAPING OF THE ELIZABETHAN CHURCH

Circling back to 1570, the people could see that there was increasing clarity in the policies of the established Church. They may also have begun to discern Elizabeth's vision for the English Church, illustrated by her treatment of Catholics. She and her bishops focused on actions—attending public worship—rather than private beliefs. In the case of the Catholics, this approach led to harsh penalties against recusants, while church papists were typically ignored since

10. Collinson, *Puritan* Movement, 391–96.

they did attend church. This approach led to the creation of a diverse Church of England that built on the diversity initiated by Cranmer's insistence that the best way to introduce Protestantism was through worship rather than doctrine. As noted earlier, he believed that "right worship" would lead to "right beliefs:" not taking into consideration the people's application of their own filters to their worship experiences; not realizing that life experience in general and previous religious formation in particular might lead to different interpretations of the words and actions of worship according to the *Book of Common Prayer*.

However, there were some precepts that those in authority saw as non-negotiable. These included specific aspects of the polity or governance of the Church, including the continuing authority of bishops, Parliament, and the Crown. A convocation was held in 1571, where those present were required to subscribe to the Royal Supremacy and the Thirty-Nine Articles, revised and approved by Parliament since being initially approved during the convocation of 1563. One bishop, Cheyney of Gloucester, left the convocation rather than subscribe to the Thirty-Nine Articles. Remarkably, he seems not to have suffered any consequences for his actions, perhaps because they were grounded in his beliefs. He objected to the article concerning acceptable eucharistic theologies, which included the Lutheran understanding of the real presence of Christ in the eucharistic elements, Cranmer and Calvin's belief in the spiritual presence of Christ, and Zwingli's belief that the Eucharist was a commemoration of the Last Supper but did not include transubstantiation.[11]

There was no need for parishioners to reveal to anyone their beliefs concerning the Eucharist (or any of their other beliefs), as long as they attended worship. However, there

11. Hardwick, *History of the Articles of Religion*, 329–31.

were still a number of challenges facing parish priests, as Elizabethan Protestantism became somewhat more clearly defined. In some sections of the country, some parishioners disrupted services by, for instance, walking and talking loudly in front of the pulpit during the sermon. Others disrupted services by creating a chaotic situation in the church during worship, such as physically fighting over an assigned seat in a pew. These were all actions, and Elizabeth did care about them. Meanwhile, some clergy tried to push the boundaries of acceptable worship as defined in the *Book of Common Prayer* by supporting a more "lively" style of worship, including prayers not included in the *Prayer Book,* or even preaching inspired sermons that were not read from a book or given by a priest with a royal license to preach. There was quite a struggle between Archbishop John Whitgift and the more radically Protestant clergy concerning this "liveliness" in worship. Whitgift insisted on the efficacy of *Prayer Book* prayers and sermons read from the *Books of Homilies*, while many preferred (and opted for) extemporaneous prayers and sermons.

These more radical Protestant clergy exerted pressure to continue reforming the Elizabethan Church. The Scriptures were their guide as they pressed for simpler, more extemporaneous worship. Often, but not always, they were supported by their parishioners in introducing variations in worship that deviated from the *Book of Common Prayer.* This was illegal, but it did happen. Priests in Elizabethan England were constantly negotiating the space that defined acceptable worship, and pressure from the Calvinists had an effect over time.

As the Elizabethan Church matured, so did its theological underpinnings (as had been true in the early Church). Most notably, by the end of Elizabeth's reign, Richard Hooker was busy examining the scriptural foundation of English belief and practice. He began his most significant work, *Of the Laws of Ecclesiastical Polity*, by asserting "the sacred authority of scripture," and going on to declare, "these scriptures . . . lay before us all the duties which God requires . . . as necessary . . . [for] salvation." He then discusses the problem of conflicting texts, reminding his readers the Bible was written for a particular purpose at a particular time. The particularity of the origin of each book, then, resulted in its containing the portion of God's truth applicable to the context of each book. Thus, he continued, all of Scripture must be considered when attempting to discern God's truth. He then went beyond the authority of Scripture, to allow rites and ceremonies that were not explicitly prohibited by Scripture.[12]

Throughout Elizabeth's reign, her Church worked to create an identity that distinguished itself from Catholicism (which also had bishops and a very similar eucharistic liturgy), on the one hand, and the most extreme Protestants (with their emphasis on the Scriptures and worship inspired by Calvin's Geneva), on the other. In the end (that is, by 1603), it had partially succeeded. The boundary between Catholicism and Elizabethan Protestantism was well-defined. There were bishops who held authority over the parishes and clergy in their several dioceses, and all ordained ministers were required to wear certain vestments when leading services. However, the liturgy was in English, and the eucharistic theology was largely left to the interpretation of the parishioners and their clergy with diversity being the watchword. Meanwhile, the influence of Calvinism had clearly been greater than that of Catholicism, despite the bishops and rules concerning vestments.

By the 1590s, many churches across the realm were looking more and more Calvinist (or Puritan), with John

12. Hooker, *Of the Laws of Ecclesiastical Polity*, 113–14.

Foxe's *Book of Martyrs* and a large volume of the Bible prominently positioned and secured with chains within the worship space. (They were also supposed to have a copy of Erasmus's *Paraphrases of the Gospels* in English, although this volume was lacking in many parishes.) Psalms were sung *a cappella* and very slowly in the Calvinist manner, with each syllable or note being held for four slow beats, followed by a breath. Additionally, the worship space was dominated by a large pulpit located within the nave where the people would be able to hear the preacher clearly. The whitewashed walls were adorned with Scripture passages, including the Ten Commandments, the Lord's Prayer, and portions of Psalms. However, they frequently also prominently displayed the Queen's Arms, as incongruous as that may seem. This description did not apply to all parish churches, but by the end of Elizabeth's reign, it was the norm. In a few instances, the chancel had also been modified to accommodate communicants receiving Communion either seated or kneeling. In these cases, pews with or without kneelers were added, forming a U within the chancel with the Communion table in the middle of this U. In contrast, in some churches (and especially in private chapels on large estates), worship spaces reflected the growing popularity among the elite for Italianate decorations, furnishings, and paintings. However, Calvinist worship spaces dominated Elizabeth's reign as it came to an end on March 24, 1603. Meanwhile, official religious policy was anything but clear. The Elizabethan Reformation thrived on ambiguity. That was a way to minimize dispute. So, it is not surprising that over the course of Elizabeth's forty-three-year reign ambiguities compounded previous ambiguities, and few were resolved. That inherent messiness of religious policy was then made worse by the continuing challenges posed by Catholics and Puritans. Much remained unresolved when Elizabeth died.

DISCUSSION QUESTIONS

1. Why do you think it took ten years for England to really return to Protestantism after Elizabeth I became queen?

2. How important were the Marian exiles in the rise of Puritanism in England during Elizabeth's reign?

3. In what ways was Elizabeth's rule more sophisticated and effective that the other Tudor monarchs?

4. Why was it so hard for Elizabeth and her bishops to control Catholicism and Puritanism while establishing their version of Protestantism?

6

THE STORY CONTINUES

(1603–Present)

So, how did the Church get from what it was when
Elizabeth died to what it is today? Yes, then it was the
English Church, the Church of England, and now we're focusing on the Anglican and Episcopal Churches around the
world. But what has influenced the changes that have led to
the current Church over the past four-plus centuries? Five
separate developments stand out:

- The dis-establishment of the Church of England and
  a decade of religious confusion, including radical religions in the mid-seventeenth century, followed by the
  restoration of the established Church;

- The Oxford (and to some extent the Cambridge)
  Movement of the nineteenth century, which reclaimed

some beliefs and practices, as well as architecture, from the medieval Church;

- The founding of Churches connected to the Church of England around the world and the creation of the Anglican Communion later in the nineteenth century;

- The twentieth-century liturgical renewal movement, which began in the 1930s and culminated in changes in liturgy around the world; and

- The rise of multiple challenges, ranging from changes in the roles of women and transgendered people to racism and climate change.

Additionally, this chapter will continue, as in the previous chapters, to identify ways in which English religion was affected by continental reform, the role of the laity in changing English religion, and ultimately, why Anglican and Episcopal Churches of the twenty-first century look the way they do.

James VI of Scotland became James I of England following Elizabeth I's death in 1603. He was the son of Mary, queen of Scots, and Elizabeth's cousin, but more importantly, he was a theologian, as well as a monarch. His dream was the reunion of all of Christendom, and this dream would lead to some changes in the English Church but would also weaken the monarchy (given some of his decisions and his clumsy monarchical style). Early in his reign, he convened the Hampton Court Conference in response to the challenge of the more radical Protestants, both clergy and lay. This conference had a huge impact on the Church going forward. It was at this conference that James powerfully supported the role of bishops in the hierarchy of the Church with the words, "no bishop, no king." This conference also approved a slightly modified *Prayer Book* and initiated the process that would lead to the creation of a new translation of the Bible into the fast-evolving English language of the early seventeenth century: "The King James Version" or the Authorized Version of the Bible. The minimal changes in the *Prayer Book* were disappointing to the Calvinists in England. The new Bible was a monumental contribution to the Christian faith.

James's second son, Charles, succeeded him as Charles I in 1525, due to the premature death of James's eldest son, Henry in 1618. Charles's reign was a disaster. It was marked by both religious and economic tensions, as well as by his attempts to rule without Parliament. In terms of religion, his selection of William Laud as archbishop of Canterbury substantially increased tensions with radical Protestants, including Puritans of various stripes. Laud believed in the "beauty of holiness" and ordered all churches to return their altars to their traditional position against the east wall and to install communion rails (supposedly to keep dogs away from the altar). He also encouraged the introduction of other decorations. These developments all influenced the appearance of churches and would, some two centuries later, influence changes introduced by the Oxford and Cambridge Movements.

RELIGIOUS CONFUSION AND ITS EFFECTS ON THE SEVENTEENTH-CENTURY CHURCH

The tensions resulting from Laud's policies and those of Charles I in turning his back on Parliament to rule alone (plus other challenges), ultimately led to the English Civil Wars, which consumed much of England from 1642 to 1649. During this time there were two Civil Wars, one after the other. Religion was certainly both one of the causes and an effect of these wars. Additionally, substantial numbers of Puritans were among those who saw these wars as a way to reform religion in a Calvinist direction and most were members of the laity.

Near the end of the first Civil War, in January 1645, Parliament—that is, the House of Commons—convened (without the king) and voted to outlaw the *Book of Common Prayer*, replacing it with the Calvinist *Directory for the Public Worship of God* (approved the previous year by Parliament for use by the Presbyterian Church of Scotland). However, this did not end the use of the *Prayer Book* in English worship services. As was the case during the Reformation in Edward VI's and Elizabeth I's reigns, some congregations continued as they had before and just did not share the fact publicly. If the parish clergy and parishioners agreed, they could easily hide their actions. The following October, the Parliament abolished bishops, archbishops, and cathedrals, replacing them with a presbyterian form of governance. However, this did not result in bishops vanishing from the realm. The Church of England had been disestablished, but bishops still ordained new priests, although this was done in secret. In many places parishioners continued to attend services and both clergy and laypeople continued to minister to the needs of those in their communities, without anyone asserting authority over them.

The second Civil War followed the first and ended with the execution of the king for treason in 1649, an astounding and unprecedented action, given that he had been anointed to rule in God's name. (Archbishop Laud had been executed for treason four years earlier.) Over the next decade England experimented with, first, a republican form of government, and then from December 1653 to May 1659, a protectorate with Oliver Cromwell as the lord protector for most of that time. This, plus the changes made by Parliament during the wars had a profound effect on English religion. Denominations, other than the Church of England quickly emerged, including the Presbyterians, Independents, and Baptists. The Presbyterians, who had been around since at least 1570 in England, believed in a less-hierarchical church, a church without bishops. They dominated religion in England beginning during the first half of 1646. The Independents were Calvinists like the Presbyterians. However, they believed that each congregation should govern itself independently and were the precursor of the modern United Church of Christ. Meanwhile, Baptists believed in adult or believer's baptism, since they believed that infant baptism didn't count because an infant couldn't comprehend the meaning of this rite. However, from the perspective of those who were not Baptists, adult baptism was seen as resulting in *re*-baptizing people who had been baptized as infants, and that was forbidden. The time of republican governance marked the beginning of these denominations.

The English Church at this time was led by a combination of Presbyterians and Congregationalists, as well as more traditional Church of England ministers, but not bishops. There was much contention over official religious policy, and the worship experiences of parishioners could vary quite dramatically. Ministers sometimes used portions of the forbidden *Book of Common Prayer* in combination with extemporized prayers or prayers they had written. More conforming ministers, on the other hand, used the approved Calvinist *Directory for the Public Worship of God,* although not necessarily without alteration. That being said, the worship experience of parishioners was still familiar, grounded as it was in earlier traditions combined with some suggested reforms. Yes, there was innovation and improvisation, but it was still recognizable as the Church of England.[1]

1. Milton, *England's Second Reformation,* 378.

Several radical religions also emerged during the 1650s, and they would cast a shadow over English religion later in that century and into the next. They included the Diggers, Quakers, and Ranters, among others. These groups all affirmed millenarianism, the belief that the end of time, the final judgment, was coming soon. The prevalence of this belief may have been influenced by the earth-shaking execution of the sitting, anointed monarch, Charles I, and was grounded in an interpretation of the Book of Revelation, that there would soon be a fundamental transformation of society, after which "all things will be changed." This belief manifested itself differently in different radical groups. The Diggers believed in communal sharing of food and possessions, including land. They planted crops and shared their produce. They tried to create a utopian society a little like the one in Thomas More's book which introduced the term. Ultimately, however, they threatened landowners, and the authorities shut them down.

The Quakers, on the other hand, eventually were accepted as a denomination and continue to this day. They began in the late 1640s and were most radical during the 1650s. They were led by the son of a Leicestershire weaver, George Fox, and a Yorkshire gentlewoman, Margaret Fell of Swarthmore Hall. These two collaborated in leading the movement and complimented each other in what they contributed. Fox developed the theology espoused by the Quakers, while Fell, and initially her husband, Thomas, a member of Parliament and a judge, contributed legal protection, funding, and organization to the movement. Swarthmore Hall became the communications hub of this movement.

The Quakers believed the divine spark—the Light of Christ—dwelt within each individual. This spark caused the individual to shiver or "quake," a sign that they were inspired to preach (hence their name, "Quaker"). As a part of this belief, they considered preachers (and their sermons) licensed by the Crown to be suspect. Only people inspired to preach by their inner light were seen as authentic preachers. Fox and Fell sent pairs of their followers, both women and men, into homes in communities across England and beyond to preach sermons inspired by the divine spark within, and both women and men were present to hear them. The indwelling of the Light of Christ was seen by those within the movement as temporarily removing gender from the individual who then was moved to speak. However, those outside the movement saw women's speaking during Quaker worship as scandalous and ultimately as illegal. As a result, numerous women were imprisoned for speaking in this way.[2] However, that was not the only cause of imprisonment of Quakers.

Early in the 1650s, the Quakers attracted the attention of numerous men and women, including James Naylor, who then joined the movement. Naylor soon gained notoriety when he rode into Bristol, nude and mounted on a horse while other Quakers tossed garments in front of him and acclaimed him as "Lord." This resulted in his arrest for blasphemy, and part of his punishment was to, once again, ride into Bristol on a horse, but this time to be clothed and mounted backwards, that is, facing the rear of the horse, a humiliating punishment. Others within the movement disrupted suspect sermons, often parading back and forth in front of the pulpit in the nude. In fact, nudity seems to have been an important form of protest in those early years, and unlike the other more radical religions, the Quakers spent some of their time and energy attempting to reform the more conventional denominations with their protests.

2. Peters, *Print Culture and the Early Quakers*, 128–35.

Margaret Fell and George Fox would eventually marry in 1669. Some years later, they negotiated a set of rules that the Quakers agreed to follow, creating a calm and respectable religion that would ultimately prove acceptable to the Crown. These rules included prohibiting disruptive protests, and perhaps most notably, restricting women's preaching to women's-only meetings. There would be no more women's preaching to groups that included both men and women, a curtailment of women's previous role within the movement.[3] Meanwhile, the Quakers—both men and women—were prolific letter-writers and pamphleteers who published widely, spreading their ideas throughout England and beyond.[4]

The Quakers, though, were not the most radical of the religious movements during this period. The Ranters may deserve that designation. They believed the end of the world was imminent, and that they had been chosen by God as members of the elect (that is, those chosen by God to be saved). Therefore, their worship was always a celebration of their election, which they believed also exempted them from punishment for acts that were otherwise deemed illegal. Essentially, their worship was a wild party with ranting (a precursor of modern-day rap), lots of alcohol, and profligate sex.[5]

The Church of England was re-established as the state-sponsored religion of the realm in 1660, when the protectorate collapsed following Oliver Cromwell's death. The monarchy was restored with Charles II (Charles I's eldest son) as king. All radical religions were outlawed (including for some time, the Quakers). The Presbyterians, Independents, and Baptists were allowed to continue to

---

3 Peters, "'Women's Speaking Justified,'" 205–34.

4. Peters, *Print Culture and the Early Quakers*, 1–42.

5. McGregor, "Seekers and Ranters," 121–39.

exist, although with some restrictions. The new *Prayer Book* of 1662 followed. In this *Book* the word "minister" (used since 1552) was replaced with "priest" and the language was updated to reflect common English usage of the day. It is still the official book defining worship for the Church of England, although there have been a series of authorized worship books with a variety of titles introduced over recent decades, both in England and throughout the Anglican Communion.

More importantly, however, the re-established Church of England of the late seventeenth century worked to ensure that none of the characteristics of radical religion gained a foothold in the English Church going forward. In this way, considerable numbers of lay people who had enthusiastically participated in radical religions inadvertently influenced those in authority to make sure such religious fervor could never again exist. The presence of apparently uncontrolled emotion had frightened the established Church, and those in authority took steps to ensure they never again had to contend with either such emotion or enthusiasm in worship. The result was calm, restrained worship with no possibility of excitement or any other emotion manifesting itself. This effort was aided and undergirded by the emerging Enlightenment movement, which gave pride of place to reason over emotion. The Great Awakening and the rise of Methodism in the next century, with their enthusiastic incorporation of emotion, would challenge this conventional worship. However, the Church in England emphasized strict *Prayer Book* worship to counter the pressures of that movement. The very staid Church of England indeed continued, even in North America and Ireland.

THE OXFORD AND CAMBRIDGE MOVEMENTS

Following the re-establishment of the Church of England with its resulting calm liturgical style, the next set of developments significantly affecting the Church were the Oxford and Cambridge Movements. These movements started in the 1830s within each of these universities in England. The Oxford Movement was led by John Keble and Edward Bouvarie Pusey, who would remain in the Church of England, and by John Henry Newman, who would leave the English Church for the Roman Catholic Church. It focused on reclaiming aspects of medieval religious beliefs and practices they felt had value but had been discarded during the sixteenth-century Reformation. These included belief in Christ's real presence in the bread and the wine of the Eucharist (often manifesting itself as an affirmation of transubstantiation) and in the transformational power of baptism. They also included prayers for the dead and the importance of the Eucharist as the main worship service on Sunday mornings. Anglo-Catholicism arose from these beliefs, and more generally, this movement resulted in distinctions between "High" (Anglo-Catholic) and "Low" (Evangelical) Church, based on liturgical styles. Thus, High Church people embraced more elaborate liturgies (and more of the medieval reclamations) while Low Church folk favored a simpler liturgy and gospel-based rational orthodoxy where Scripture determined right worship.

The Cambridge Movement was the liturgical and architectural response to the Oxford Movement. Led by a group of scholars based at Trinity College, Cambridge, it combined fourteenth- and fifteenth-century Gothic architecture with sixteenth- and seventeenth-century theology. In both England and the United States, it led to the building or rebuilding of churches in the neo-Gothic style reminiscent of medieval church architecture. This architecture provided spaces conducive to the return of medieval beliefs and practices, manifested in more elaborate liturgies led by clergy wearing more elaborate vestments (e.g., surplices, cassocks, chasubles, dalmatics, copes, etc.) and vested choirs. In some places, men and boys choirs, which had been common in the pre-Reformation Church, were re-established. In addition, hymn singing, which had not previously been a regular part of worship in England or North America, was introduced. (Previously, since the sixteenth-century Reformation, psalms had been the only thing the congregation sang. However, Evangelical churches had included hymns in their worship during the previous century.)[6] Architectural examples of the results of this movement in the United States include Calvary Episcopal Church in Pittsburgh, the National Cathedral in Washington, DC, and many other churches in New England and the Midwest in the United States.

THE CREATION OF THE ANGLICAN COMMUNION

England began establishing colonies in the sixteenth century when Ireland became a colony, and soon after that it began colonizing North America. The colonization of Australia came next. Then in the nineteenth century, the British Empire expanded onto every continent including Southeast Asia and Africa, and wherever the British government went, the Church of England, or at least one of the English missionary societies, went too. Similarly, as the United States

6. Ward, *A History of Global Anglicanism*, 39–40.

grew in power and prestige, it too established colonies. All of these were then places where Anglican missionaries worked to spread their faith. In particular, they spread Evangelical, that is, Bible-based, Protestant Christianity.[7] In the English colonies this led to the planting of local versions of the Church of England, even though the missionaries may not have seen that particular Church as their reason for being. Certainly, the Church Missionary Society, which was most active in the British colonies, focused primarily on converting the indigenous people of the many colonies to Christianity more broadly construed, rather than to make them members of the Church of England. And in the process the missionaries inculcated the local people with their particular form of Bible-based English Evangelical Protestant Christianity. The result was that most of the colonial churches established during the intentional spread of the British Empire were more Evangelical than the Church of England. This emphasis on Bible-based Evangelical Christianity, combined with changing cultural differences that increased the disparity between cultures, would eventually lead to tensions between the Anglican churches of the global South and those of the North.

Colonists began arriving in North America at the beginning of the seventeenth century, just as Elizabethan Protestantism was becoming the settled religion of England. In fact, colonization of North America coincided with the establishment of Protestantism in England during Elizabeth's reign and those of James I and VI and his sons. Subsequently, the successful conclusion of the American Revolution in the North American colonies cut the Church of England in America off from the English Church. In 1786, representatives from each state were invited to come

7. "Evangelical" is used in this book to describe a Bible-based religion.

to a General Convention in Philadelphia, where they wrote a constitution but were able to accomplish little else, since only the mid-Atlantic and Southern states participated. They met again three years later, and eventually were joined by the New England states. The main stumbling block for the New England states was their preference for bishops over the laity to lead the church.

This Convention added some canons (or Church laws) to the governance of the church and approved a *Book of Common Prayer*, based largely on the English *Prayer Book* of 1662. The key differences in the *Prayer Book* were the elimination of prayers for the monarch and the inclusion of the invocation of the Holy Spirit in the "Prayer of Consecration" in the Rite of Holy Communion. This change was based on an agreement between the Scottish bishops who had consecrated Samuel Seabury as the bishop of Connecticut and Seabury himself. This invocation had been missing from the *Books of Common Prayer* since 1552.[8]

The constitution of the Protestant Episcopal Church of the United States defined the governance for the new Church and created a Church that was national but not tied in any way to the government of the new United States of America. In the words of the noted historian of Anglicanism Kevin Ward, this was "a kind of establishment without establishment."[9] It called for a General Convention to meet every three years. Each state was to elect a deputation to the General Convention, comprising no more than four clergy and four laymen, and each deputation would have one vote. Duly consecrated bishops were to have jurisdiction in the states where they lived. They were also permitted to confirm and ordain in states without bishops and would meet

8. Chorley, "The General Conventions," 246–65; Scott, "The House of Deputies," 22–23.

9. Ward, *A History of Global Anglicanism*, 65.

as the House of Bishops, while the lay and clerical deputies would meet together—but separate from the bishops—as the House of Deputies. (The creation of the House of Deputies was included in the original constitution in 1786; the House of Bishops was added in 1789.) A major innovation in creating this new Church was that clergy and lay members of the House of Deputies had equal authority with bishops in the governance of the Church. Furthermore, the clergy and laity who were members of the Convention were to be called deputies, not delegates. They were not to represent their states, but rather to be fully independent, well-informed participants, open to the guidance of the Holy Spirit and engaged in working for the best interests of the Church at large.[10] The House of Deputies would have a president. The senior bishop would be designated the presiding bishop and would preside over the House of Bishops as first among equals. Years later, in 1926, the constitution was changed, and the presiding bishop was elected, initially for a twelve-year term and later for a nine-year term. However, the presiding bishop would have very little authority. That rested primarily in the General Convention.

Shortly after the American Revolution, in 1788, England began shipping convicts, especially those from debtors' prisons to Australia. Previously such convicts had been sent to settle the North American colony of Georgia, but the American Revolution had ended that option. Gradually, the population in Australia increased beyond the bounds of the penal colonies and included both more settlers and priests. They established churches and were overseen by the bishop of London, who had also been the bishop to the North American colonies until the American Revolution. Then in 1814 Australia was put under the purview of the new Diocese of Calcutta, and in 1836 the Diocese of Australia was

10. Anderson, "The Role of a Deputy."

established with William Grant Broughton as its bishop. However, whereas most British colonization included missionary work with the indigenous people of the region, that was not the case in Australia. Rather, colonization and the founding of churches was focused on the English settlers and not the indigenous people. Further, the English settlers were grouped regionally with Sydney, Melbourne, and some other areas being dominated by Evangelicals, while in other regions, especially South Australia and West Australia, Anglo-Catholicism held sway. There was no coherent nation Church; rather, regionalism prevailed. This may explain the fact that the Australian Church did not develop a constitution until 1959 and did not gain autonomy from the English Church until 1962.[11]

Meanwhile, Christianity initially came to Australia's neighbor, New Zealand via the Church Missionary Society, which sent a mission to convert the Māori people in 1814 and did at least part of their teaching in the Māori language. Christianity spread throughout this country, and the Māori people were enthusiastic evangelists. By 1840 colonists had arrived from England and Scotland. They established Anglican churches, and George Augustus Selwyn was soon made bishop of New Zealand. However, as would be true for colonists in other places, the settlers wanted their familiar Church in this new place but without ties to the government. The *Book of Common Prayer* (*Te Rawiri* in Māori), which was based on the English *Prayer Book* of 1662, was their focus. In 1857, they created a constitution and thus became autonomous from the Church of England. Subsequently, as the country grew the Diocese of New Zealand was divided into multiple dioceses and by the late twentieth

11. Ward, *A History of Global Anglicanism*, 275–86; "Anglican Church of Australia," https//:www.britannica.com/topic/Anglican -Church-of-Australia.

century the Māori people had moved out of the shadows and were recognized as an important part of the Church along with the Diocese of Polynesia, which had begun as a missionary diocese of New Zealand. The constitution of the Church was revised in 1992 creating the Anglican Church of Aotearoa, New Zealand, and Polynesia, recognizing the three cultures that comprise the Church in New Zealand.[12] Late in 1989, *A New Zealand Prayerbook* was published, which has since provided much spiritual nurture to people around the world.

Prior to the American Revolution colonists settled in some of the areas of North America now known as Canada, but most of them were French and Roman Catholic, as were the missionaries initially working with the First Nation peoples of that region. However, as a result of the Revolution, numerous priests and laypeople who favored the British moved north and the Church Missionary Society got involved in bringing the First Nation peoples to Anglicanism. And so, as in New Zealand, the Anglican Church of Canada was a result of the work of missionaries, plus the efforts of settlers. However, the First Nation people were not treated with the respect accorded the aboriginal people of New Zealand, and the Anglican Church of Canada has only recently apologized for the way they treated the First Nation people.[13]

In other parts of the world, the English were not the first colonists to arrive. In many parts of Africa, for instance, the French, Germans, Dutch, and Portuguese had arrived earlier, bringing with them Roman Catholicism, Lutheranism, or Dutch Reformed Christianity. Additionally,

12. Ward, *A History of Global Anglicanism*, 286–90; "Anglican Church in Aotearoa, New Zealand and Polynesia," https://www.anglican.org.nz/About/History.

13. Ward, *A History of Global Anglicanism*, 68–82.

throughout much of the rest of Africa and Southern Asia, Islam had become dominant. An exception was Sierra Leone, the center of the slave trade between Africa and North America. There, the Society for the Propagation of the Gospel (an English Evangelical mission society) arrived in the mid-eighteenth century to bring Christianity to both the slave traders and the slaves. Indigenous leaders there emerged to create a dynamic Church.

In other regions the story is complex. The various English missionary societies, including the Church Missionary Society, the Society for the Propagation of the Gospel, and the Universities' Mission to Central Africa, worked to establish Anglican Churches with varying degrees of success. Sometimes, as in India, they were linked to the ruling elite, while at other times and in other places they successfully involved the indigenous people in the leadership as well as in the membership of the new Churches. In the twenty-first century, Anglican Churches in two countries stand out and stand in sharp contrast to one another: The Church of Nigeria and the Church of Kenya. The Nigerian Church is huge and still growing at an impressive rate. It is strongly Evangelical and conservative. Meanwhile, the Church of Kenya, which owes its founding to a combination of missionary societies—the Universities' Mission to Central Africa and the Church Missionary Society—was influenced by the East African Revival Movement and is much more open to the involvement of women, including ordaining them to the priesthood almost ten years before the English Church did so.[14]

British colonization was not the only origin of global Anglicanism. Missionaries from the Episcopal Church in the United States also created Anglican Churches. These included the Anglican Churches in Japan, Mexico, and the

14. Ward, *A History of Global Anglicanism*, 132, 190.

Philippines. In Mexico, a group of disaffected Roman Catholics asked for support from the Diocese of New York in the Episcopal Church of the United States. Virginia Theological Seminary, then a bastion of Evangelicalism, also got involved in Mexico and elsewhere. Additionally, several Latin American Anglican Churches owed their founding to the South American Missionary Society, which originated in the United States and sought to bring Christianity to South American Indians.[15]

Looking more particularly at Anglicanism in North America and England, in the nineteenth century ecumenism and the related desire for greater self-definition within denominations led the leaders of the Episcopal Church to reach out to Anglican Churches in other parts of the world. This led to the creation of the Anglican Communion. Initially, this network of churches from around the world was defined by beliefs contained in a document approved by the General Convention of the Episcopal Church meeting in Chicago in 1886, where the lay and clergy deputies, along with the bishops, had agreed on the wording. Two years later, after some minor modifications, it was approved by the Anglican bishops and archbishops from around the world, including those mentioned above, gathered for the Lambeth Conference in England. Titled the Chicago-Lambeth Quadrilateral, this document listed the following basic characteristics of global Anglicanism:

- Holy Scriptures of the Old and New Testaments are the revealed Word of God, contain all things necessary for salvation, and are the rule and ultimate standard of faith.

15. Kater, "Latin American Anglicanism," 1–27; Ward, *A History of Global Anglicanism*, 102–5.

- The Apostles Creed, as the baptismal symbol, and the Nicene Creed are the sufficient statement of faith.

- There are two sacraments, established by Christ: baptism and Eucharist.

- The historic episcopate (that is, the position of bishop), is key to unity.

The result was the creation of the worldwide Anglican Communion. It was conceived as a network of Churches that looked to one another for support. They primarily saw their origin in the Church of England and in England's policies of colonization. The bishops and archbishops from the various churches (or provinces) that made up the Anglican Communion meet every ten years in the Lambeth Conference where they provide mutual support and sometimes issue non-binding theological statements concerning matters of cultural importance.

Just over a century after its founding, some churches in the Anglican Communion tried to claim unprecedented authority for the Communion as they unsuccessfully attempted to remove the Episcopal Church from the Communion for approving the election and ordination as bishop of New Hampshire of a partnered gay man, Gene Robinson. To complicate matter, some African and Asian archbishops did not understand the governance of the Episcopal Church, and tried to persuade the presiding bishop of the Episcopal Church, the Rt. Rev. Frank Griswold, to remove Bishop Robinson from his position as bishop diocesan. However, Griswold did not have the authority to do so.

THE TWENTIETH-CENTURY LITURGICAL RENEWAL MOVEMENT

Following the creation of the Anglican Communion, the first (very modest) revision of the *Book of Common Prayer* was approved in the United States in 1892. Another modest *Prayer Book* revision was approved in 1928, as that nation continued to change. The liturgical changes to come would be much more substantial. The Great Depression of the early 1930s planted the seeds that would create the context for the twentieth-century liturgical renewal movement. However, the real catalyst for such renewal was the discovery of ancient Christian documents (*The Apostolic Tradition* and others), dating from the second and third centuries.

In 1935, just as people were beginning to recover from the initial effects of the Great Depression, some seminarians in the United States began exploring a variety of documents that would inspire liturgical change and even liturgical renewal. Four centuries earlier, in the 1540s, Thomas Cranmer and others had studied the earliest writings of the Church known to them, those from the fifth and sixth centuries, as well as the Scriptures, as they considered how best to reform worship in England. They grounded their changes in worship in the beliefs and practices of the early Church that they saw in these writings. Similarly, twentieth-century scholars referred to writings from the early church as they pondered liturgical change. However, as a result of the recent discoveries of earlier Christian documents, the writings from the early Church now available dated from as early as the second century, way earlier than the writings available to Reformation scholars like Thomas Cranmer.

Writings dating from the second and third centuries, including the writings of Justin Martyr and *The Apostolic Tradition* of Hyppolytus, offered detailed descriptions of early baptismal rites and the Eucharist. Examining these early descriptions of the sacraments led to the realization that the Eucharist centered around taking, blessing, breaking, and giving the bread and wine. Baptism involved full immersion in the water and anointing. It centered on the declaration of the beliefs contained in the Apostles Creed. This study also revealed that in that earlier time there was much greater lay involvement than in recent centuries, and liturgical actions, including Palm Sunday Processions and the Christmas Eve midnight service, were much more dramatic than at any time since.

In 1949, the General Convention of the Episcopal Church in the United States authorized the Standing Liturgical Commission to produce a series of *Prayer Book Studies*. One such study, published in 1953, foreshadowed many of the changes that would be incorporated in the next *Book of Common Prayer*. These included providing for greater lay involvement and modifying the Eucharist by moving the breaking of the bread from the middle of the Prayer of Consecration to after the Lord's Prayer (which immediately followed the Prayer of Consecration). Also, this document suggested reintroducing the verbal exchange of the passing of the Peace (which had been absent since 1552) and relocating the Gloria to the beginning of the eucharistic rite. (It had been near the end of the service since the first *Prayer Book* in 1549. Thomas Cranmer felt it set a much too joyful tone for the Eucharist.)

The liturgical renewal movement then quickly spread to local churches. There were increasing calls for weekly celebrations of the Eucharist and for more liturgical options for Holy Week. Additionally, people wanted the presider to face the people during the celebration of the Eucharist. This, in turn, created an increased desire for re-designed chancels with altars or Communion tables pulled away from the "east" wall, so priests could stand behind them. There were also calls for more liturgical choices and more lay participation in worship.

While all of this was going on in the Episcopal Church in the United States, the liturgical renewal movement increasingly involved multiple denominations and nations. One result was the formation of specific groups, each with its own focus. The Anglican-Roman Catholic International Commission (ARCIC) focused initially on eucharistic doctrine, ordination, and issues of authority, but full cooperation fell apart when the Catholics pushed for greater involvement of the pope. The International Consultation on English Texts (ICET) was more successful. Founded in 1969, it completed its work in 1975, having developed modern English versions of the Apostles and Nicene Creeds, and the Lord's Prayer. The new creeds were widely adopted across the English-speaking world. The Lord's Prayer received less acceptance.

While this work was going on, denominations, most notably the Roman Catholics and the Episcopalians in the United States, were revising their liturgies more thoroughly. The Catholics, under the leadership of Pope John XXIII met in the Second Vatican Council in 1962 and moved from the Latin Mass to the Mass in English (using language inspired by Thomas Cranmer). Meanwhile, the Episcopalians continued to move toward a new *Prayer Book*.

In 1964, to include as many people and perspectives as possible in revising the *Prayer Book*, the General Convention revised the constitution of the Episcopal Church to allow for trial use of the draft liturgies throughout the Church in regular Sunday worship. Clergy in local parishes could apply to become "Trial Use" parishes. Initially, these draft liturgies were focused on the two sacraments. However, they soon included revisions throughout the *Prayer*

Book, and so, beginning in 1970, local congregations and their clergy began using large paperback books to guide their worship. In chronological order, these were:

- *Services for Trail Use* (of 1970, known as the "Green Book" in the localities),

- *Authorized Services* (of 1973, the "Zebra Book"),

- *Draft Proposed Prayer Book* (of 1975, the "Great Blue Whale").

After each book had been in use for a while, the participating local congregations were invited to give feedback to the Standing Liturgical Commission, which was overseeing this process of liturgical renewal. For instance, the General Confession in the "Zebra Book" included no expression of regret. This omission resulted in multiple comments from parishes and was corrected in the next book, the "Great Blue Whale."

In 1976 at what would prove to be a momentous meeting of the General Convention of the Episcopal Church in Minneapolis, the new *Book of Common Prayer* was approved almost unanimously. It would be ratified for a second time by the General Convention in 1979, without any modifications (as required by the constitution). This new book included two rites (one in traditional, Cranmerian, language and the other in contemporary English) for each of the Daily Offices and even more rites for the Eucharist. Also, a "Rite 3" eucharistic liturgy, which allowed for even more flexibility, was added, along with numerous special liturgies for special days, including Ash Wednesday, Palm Sunday, Maundy Thursday, Good Friday, and the Great Vigil of Easter. All of these liturgies for special days were inspired by rites found in those very early documents of the Church. Additional liturgical changes included the development of two separate lectionaries (or calendars of Scripture readings), one a three-year cycle for Sunday Eucharists and the other a two-year cycle for the Daily Office. (Previously, there had been a single year-long lectionary.) Also, while the first *Prayer Book* had aspired to create a liturgical conversation of sorts between the priest and the people, this new book markedly increased the level of lay participation in all services.

The other major change in the *Prayer Book* was to the Rite of Baptism, which was to become the single, consolidated Rite of Christian Initiation for the Church going forward. The rite that was Confirmation would no longer be needed and was to be eliminated. The changes were based on rites from the second century of Christianity. As part of this revision, the traditional prayer for the Sevenfold Gifts of the Spirit was moved from the Confirmation Rite to the Baptismal Rite, where it had initially been. Additionally, the Baptismal Covenant was expanded to include explicit declarations and promises previously assumed but left unstated. However, while this new Rite of Baptism was approved by the Convention, the House of Bishops successfully resisted the effort to eliminate the Rite of Confirmation, over which they always presided. Instead, they insisted that it be added back into the new *Prayer Book* (with some revisions), creating confusion among the people in the pews and their clergy, as to its reason for being, given the nature of the newly revised Baptismal Rite. However, its continued inclusion kept in place a cultural rite of passage that society and many parents of adolescents appreciated.

This liturgical renewal movement resulted in momentous changes in worship throughout the Episcopal Church, in the United States and beyond, all ultimately the work of deputies and bishops acting through the authority of the General Conventions of the Episcopal Church.

There were traditional options available, and many congregations clung to these. However, others enthusiastically embraced the new language, and perhaps especially the new Rite of Baptism, which infused many with joy and energy they had not felt in worship before. This movement contributed substantially to creating the Episcopal Church of the twenty-first century.

Meanwhile, in England where Parliament must approve any change in the *Book of Common Prayer* and refuses to do so, the Church has chosen to publish books of liturgies to guide worship in congregations, employing contemporary English and reflecting the influence of the scholarship that had dominated so many churches following the discovery of documents dating from the second and third centuries. Books with the primary title, *Common Worship* comprise "a family of volumes which, together with the *Book of Common Prayer*, make up the official liturgical resource of the Church of England."[16]

THE EMERGENCE OF MULTIPLE CHALLENGES TO ANGLICAN CHURCHES

Circling back to the early twentieth century, one of the most significant societal changes has been the changing role of women. A second and related new emphasis on gender and sexuality has also risen to prominence. Women's roles began to change in the 1870s, while attention to issues of sexuality emerged by the 1930s. Concerns regarding gender would come later.

16. "Common Worship," https://www.churchofengland.org/prayer-and-worship/worship-texts-and-resources/common-worship.

Beginning in the later years of the nineteenth century, women, at least in Europe and North America, began to speak more assertively to the Church hierarchy, but they also became increasingly indispensable in funding the work of the Church and the very existence of individual congregations. In the United States, the Women's Auxiliary of the Board of Missions of the Episcopal Church was authorized by General Convention in 1871, in an effort to capitalize on the women's movement of that century while safeguarding the dominant position of men within the Church. The women's goal was to enhance, not compete with, existing Church structures, but fundamentally, their initial role was to supplement the funding of the work of the Church in the United States. At the turn of the twentieth century, society looked to women to raise funds for special projects, both within the Church and in the broader society. Returning to the Women's Auxiliary, the first triennial meeting of this organization was held in 1874 with sixty-six women from five states in attendance. In 1889, they established the United Thank Offering (UTO), which still exists, to raise funds for Episcopal missionary work. Much later, in 1984, they became the Episcopal Church Women.

After World War I, women gained a new level of respect from men, as a result of their contributions to the war effort, and then they gained the right to vote in both England and the United States. As a result, many in the United States expected the General Convention, meeting in 1922 in Portland, Oregon, to vote to allow women to be seated as deputies; however, that would not be the case. Despite efforts to the contrary, over the next forty-five years, the Convention repeatedly voted to exclude women from the governance of the Church. World War II provided a brief hiatus when women did hold some leadership positions, but that change didn't last. There were additional challenges from women, and then in the mid-1960s, after women were denied seats again, Presiding Bishop Arthur Lichtenberger chastised the House of Deputies for taking UTO money for missionary work from the Episcopal Church Women but still explicitly excluding women from participation as deputies. In 1967, his words led to real change. The General Convention, meeting in Seattle that summer, voted to seat women as deputies of the Convention, beginning in 1970. Women could then also serve as lay readers in churches for the first time, and they could serve on parish vestries. Things were indeed changing for lay women.

Meanwhile, women were also trying to gain access to the priesthood. (They were already serving as deaconesses, albeit with limited approved functions.) There were a couple of earlier incidents, but the first woman to become a priest within the Anglican Communion was Florence Li Tim Oi, who was ordained in Hong Kong on January 25, 1944. However, her ordination was not validated by the Lambeth Conference that followed in 1948 and did not lead to the ordination to the priesthood of women in the United States or anywhere else. However, a further small step toward the ordination of women was taken in 1964, when deaconesses were allowed to marry, a right previously allowed only to (male) deacons.

Some in the United States hoped the priesting of women would come quickly after women were approved as deputies to the General Convention in 1967. However, that would not be the case—a disappointment to many. In June 1974, the call for the immediate ordination of women to the priesthood grew stronger. And yet, "immediate" action was not forthcoming. One older woman observed that it was beginning to look like the issue of the ordination of women to the priesthood would become the new perennial issue just as seating women as deputies had been the issue from

1919 to 1967. Hearing these words, Suzanne Hiatt, one of the women hoping to be ordained, said, "Instantly I realized she was right, and my vocation was not to continue to ask for permission to be a priest, but to be a priest." She and others in similar situations had run out of patience and decided to act.[17]

On July 29, 1974, at the Church of the Advocate in Philadelphia, with the future suffragan bishop of Massachusetts, Barbara Harris, serving as crucifer, eleven women were ordained to the priesthood. They were Suzanne Hiatt, Carter Heyward, Merrill Bitner, Allison Cheek, Emily Hewitt, Marie Morefield, Jeanette Pickard, Betty Bone Scheiss, Karina Welles Swanson, Nancy Hatch Wittig, and Alla Bozarth-Campbell. The ordaining bishops (none of whom were engaged in active ministry) were Daniel Corrigan, Robert DeWitt, and Edward Welles. The reaction from the hierarchy was swift and clear. Church leaders (and others) were shocked that this had happened without permission. At a meeting of the House of Bishops, held the next month, the House chastised those bishops who had participated and refused to speak to the women. The bishops were in turn denounced for their actions. Meanwhile, those who had been ordained began to serve as priests in selected locations, including as faculty at the Episcopal Divinity School in Cambridge, Massachusetts. Roughly a year later, on September 7, 1975, four more women were ordained by another retired bishop. Later that same year, the Anglican Church of Canada authorized the ordination of women to the priesthood. The stage was set for the Episcopal Church to take official action on this important policy, although women in England would have to wait until 1992 to be allowed to be ordained to the priesthood.

17. Darling, *New Wine*, 123.

Meanwhile, in the United States, in preparation for the next General Convention to be held in Minneapolis in 1976 (where a new Episcopal *Prayer Book* would first be approved), canonical lawyers determined that all that was needed to authorize the ordination of women to the priesthood in the Episcopal Church was a change to the canons of the church, which could take effect immediately. They wouldn't need to amend the constitution, which would have required a second reading at the Convention in 1979 before it would have been effective. The General Convention did pass the proposed canonical change (albeit by a very close vote), stating that the canons for admission of candidates and ordination to the three orders of ordained ministry—bishops, priests, and deacons—shall be equally applicable to both men and women. It was such a simple solution. One hundred more women were ordained by the end of 1976, and the next year, those who had been "irregularly" ordained in 1974 and 1975 were "regularized."

Early in 1977, the Conference on Women in Ministries was held in St. Louis, MO. Many of the newly ordained women were present, along with a very large number of lay women. The purpose of the conference was to underscore the fact that women were already, and had always, been engaged in forms of ministry. It further provided ways for women to experience the leadership and affirmation of other women. It was transformative for many in attendance, especially watching a woman preside at the Eucharist. Leadership involving both lay and ordained women has flourished ever since in the Episcopal Church and elsewhere in many provinces of the Anglican Communion. A multitude of laywomen serve their local parishes and communities, and there are a huge number of women currently serving as priests. Additionally, a substantial number of women now serve as bishops. From July 2006 through

2015, the presiding bishop of the Episcopal Church was The Most Rev. Katharine Jefferts Schori. The Lambeth Conferences now include women who are bishops from various (though not all) parts of the Anglican Communion.

Thus, the issue of the priesting of women and the selection or election of women as bishops has become somewhat commonplace, at least in some parts of the world. Meanwhile, a new (but related) issue has emerged. Just as the ordination of women to the priesthood was grounded in changes in the status of women in society over time, so too was the ordination of gay men and lesbians, especially those who were partnered, as well as bisexual and transgendered people, and those questioning their sexuality.

The General Convention addressed human sexuality as early as 1931, when, in talking about marital sexual relations, it asserted that

> The Spirit of God dwells in every human being and . . . therefore both body and soul are holy. It satisfies and glorifies the sexual life and the sexual relationship, and within the bonds of marriage makes it a sacramental thing.[18]

Homosexuality first surfaced as an issue in the Episcopal Church in 1974 when Integrity, the organization that supports those grappling with issues of sexuality and/or gender within the Episcopal Church, came into existence. The momentous General Convention of 1976 (that first approved the new *Prayer* Book and changed the canons to allow the ordination of women to the priesthood) approved a resolution "recognizing gay and lesbian people as children of God." It then urged the Joint Commission on the Church and Human Affairs to study in depth the issue of the ordination of

18. "Report of the Joint Commission on Marriage and Divorce," 480–81.

gay men and lesbians. Three years later, while also giving final approval to the new *Prayer Book*, the General Convention of 1979 received a report from the Joint Commission arguing that "homosexuality alone should not be a barrier to ordination" in the Episcopal Church. This assertion was resisted by the House of Bishops in that Convention and in the next (in 1982). Then in 1985, echoing the urging of the Convention in 1976, the bishops called on dioceses to find ways to improve understanding of homosexuality. This underscored the desire of the Church to foster respect for differences concerning human sexuality. Meanwhile, gay men and lesbians became increasingly visible within the Church in the United States and were increasingly accepted in many localities across the country. Furthermore, as had been true with women called to the priesthood, bishops began ordaining partnered gay men and lesbians. These developments, not surprisingly, gave rise to some negative responses, and more would follow.

Meanwhile, within the Anglican Communion, the issue of homosexuality was marked by increasingly uncompromising negative statements, although the desire to provide pastoral support for gay men and lesbians was affirmed each time. Beginning in 1978, the subject was raised in the discussion of marriage and sexuality. Ten years later, the subject of homosexuality was discussed alongside the issue of polygamy. Then in 1998, the Lambeth Conference approved a statement explicitly opposing "the legitimizing or blessing of same sex unions" and "ordaining those involved in same gender unions."[19]

Five years later, the General Convention of 2003 moved both acceptance of and resistance to homosexuality to a new level. That Convention approved the ordination of Gene Robinson, a partnered gay man elected by his diocese

19. Ward, *A History of Global Anglicanism*, 305–7.

as bishop of New Hampshire and officially began discussing the blessing of same-sex unions. Bishop Robinson's approval triggered strong criticism from across the Anglican Communion, especially in Africa and parts of Asia, as well as within the Episcopal Church.[20] Some archbishops and bishops, especially those from African Anglican churches attempted, without success, to have the Episcopal Church removed from the Anglican Communion because of Bishop Robinson's approval for ordination, and at the next Lambeth Conference after his ordination, he was excluded from attending. The seeds for this disapproval originated in the pre-Christian cultures of the Global South, combined with the teachings of Evangelical Christianity introduced by the missionaries who accompanied the Crown when founding new colonies.

Throughout the first decades of the twenty-first century, acceptance of gay men and lesbians, as well as transgendered, bisexual, and questioning people, has continued to grow throughout much of the Episcopal Church and in many of the northern provinces of the Anglican Communion; however, that has not been so in all parts of the Anglican Communion. In the United States, the ordination of such people has also become less and less remarkable. Not everyone and not every region supports this development equally, but the move toward acceptance continues to progress with surprising speed. Thus, in many places in the United States, the Episcopal Church of the twenty-first century also looks the way it does because of the open participation of gay men, lesbians, bisexual, and transgendered people, as well as those questioning their sexuality, and again, the laity were definitely involved in this development, particularly at the local level.

20. Hill, Harvey, and Watson. "In Christ There Is No Gay or Straight?," 37–68.

However, the work of the Church continues. The status of women and issues of human sexuality are certainly not the only challenges facing the Church today across the Anglican Communion. Other issues including colonialism, racism, global warming, and continuing liturgical change provide ongoing challenges with which the Church must grapple.

CONCLUSION

All the key developments in the English, and later, Anglican Churches over the period from 1600 to the present day discussed here contributed to transformations that led to the modern Anglican Church. The continental Reformations, especially reform in Switzerland, and the involvement of lay people both contributed to several of these developments, as did societal and theological changes and the discovery of ancient documents. All influenced the creation of the Church of the twenty-first century, which indeed can be characterized as embodying "diversity within unity."

DISCUSSION QUESTIONS

1. Which of the several influential things that happened between 1603 and the present was most important for the development of the Anglican Churches? Why?

2. What similarities do you see between the processes that created the first *Prayer Book* in England and the most recent one in the United States? What are the greatest differences between the two processes?

3. What are the biggest differences between the Church at the end of Elizabeth I's reign and the Church of today?

CONCLUSION

THIS STORY BEGAN WITH papal challenges, the Black Death, and Renaissance humanism. It described events that spanned over four centuries and ended with the challenges facing the Anglican Communion today. At three key points, Church leaders looked back to find inspiration for liturgical change in the Church. In the midst of the Reformation, during the reign of Edward VI, Thomas Cranmer and others looked to writings from the early Church, which at the time were the Scriptures and works originating in the fourth and fifth centuries. In the early nineteen century, scholars at Oxford looked back to those same writings to determine what of value might have been overlooked during the Reformation. Then, in the mid-twentieth century, seminarians and Church leaders, alike, once again turned to the early Church for inspiration. However, this time the writings that would inspire liturgical renewal would come from the second and third centuries, thanks to more recent manuscript discoveries. In two instances, the result was a new *Book of Common Prayer*. In the first instance, the *Prayer Books* completed in

1549 and 1552; in the second, the Episcopal *Prayer Book* of 1979 and other books of worship, and additional liturgical works published since.

Between 1520 and 1603, the English people and their churches dealt with multiple changes in the religion of the realm, and the experience was different in each locality. Similar momentous changes were occurring on the continent during this same time, and the continental Reformations played a huge role in the development of Protestantism in England. Ultimately, at least in England, it seems that those eighty years or so did not create a new, settled religion, but rather, began a process that would continue, in some places up to the present day.

The advent of Protestantism in England came in the form of books read and discussed by university students and stories of life experiences shared by merchants and seamen who worshipped at Lutheran or Protestant churches when their work took them periodically to the continent. Next came Henry VIII's break with Rome and the papacy, and the work of key leaders to introduce Lutheran beliefs into official religion in England. Then, after a few years of conservative backlash in the religion of the Crown, the Calvinist boy king, Edward VI, succeeded his father as king, and Archbishop Thomas Cranmer began to introduce Protestant worship, and thereby, beliefs, into the realm. Over the next six years, England became increasingly radically Protestant. However, these developments were cut short by Edward's death and the accession of his sister, Mary I, a lifelong Catholic, to the Crown. She did her best to restore Catholicism in England, but she ran out of time, dying after a five-year reign. Ann Boleyn's daughter, Elizabeth I, then became queen and reigned long enough to see acceptance of Protestantism grow appreciably. However, the processes of religious change did not suddenly end when Elizabeth died. Rather, arguments over religion in general and forms of Protestantism, in particular, were still gaining strength.

In the focus on sixteenth-century religious change, this story has used official religious policy as a backdrop for the actions of priests and lay people in local parishes. Some enthusiastically embraced the new religion of Protestantism rather quickly. However, reluctance marked the response of most: reluctance to turn away from familiar forms of piety and beliefs; reluctance to change their religion. Nevertheless, men and women living through these times ultimately declared their faith (or their opposition to others' faiths) through their actions, their wills, and their publications. In these ways they shaped their own religious identities, whether self-consciously or in response to the exigencies of the time. This was true in the sixteenth century but also in the seventeenth century and beyond. Meanwhile, Protestantism gradually gained acceptance during the later years of Elizabeth's reign, and indeed, England was a Protestant nation by 1603. Yet, that doesn't mean it was as fully Protestant as many wanted. After all, there were still bishops, and the range of styles of worship was quite broad, ranging from Calvinist to worship reminiscent of Catholicism, too broad for many. The historic nature of the events of the sixteenth century would reverberate through at least the next five hundred years. Most significantly, thanks to the decision to change religion by first changing liturgy and the ongoing experience of individual religious identity-formation, the Church that continues to be created by these processes is most clearly known as a liturgical Church marked by its diversity within the unifying structure provided by the Church of each country, throughout the Anglican Communion. As the former presiding bishop of the Episcopal Church, Frank Griswold, has said, if you want to know what Episcopalians believe, "Come and see": come and worship with us.

The English Reformation may have begun as a series of course corrections to medieval European Christianity, but it resulted in the creation of a broad form of Protestantism in England within the Church of England and also gave birth to a number of other Protestant denominations. Further, it proved to be a catalyst for continuing religious change in the following centuries within both the Church of England, and Anglican and Episcopal Churches around the world. Having opened "Pandora's Box," there was no going back.

BIBLIOGRAPHY

Anderson, Bonnie. "The Role of a Deputy." The Episcopal Church Center, General Convention Office, 2012. https://www.episcopal church.org/phod.htm.

Baskerville, B. "The Dispossessed Religious of Gloucestershire." In *Gloucestershire Studies*, edited by H. P. R. Finberg, 63–80. Leicester, UK: Leicester University Press, 1957.

"Bonner's Articles," *VAI*, vol. II, 1536–1558, Item XLVIII.

Bradford, John. *The Writings of John Bradford*. Edited by A. Townsend. 2 vols. Cambridge: Cambridge University Press, 1853.

Brigden, Susan. *London and the Reformation*. Oxford: Oxford University Press, 1989.

Chorley, E. C., "The General Conventions of 1785, 1786 and 1789." *Historical Magazine of the Protestant Episcopal Church* 4.4 (1935) 246–65. https://www.jstor.org/stable/42968572.

Collinson, Patrick. *The Elizabethan Puritan Movement*. Berkeley, CA: University of California Press, 1967.

Coulton, Barbara. "The Establishment of Protestantism in a Provincial Town: A Study of Shrewsbury in the Sixteenth Century." *The Sixteenth Century Journal* 27.2 (1996) 307–35. http://www.jstor. com/stable/2544135.

Craig, John. "Reformers, Conflict, and Revisionism: The Reformation in Sixteenth-century Hadleigh." *The Historical Journal* 42.1 (1999) 1–23.

Craig, John, and Caroline Litzenberger. "Wills as Religious Propaganda: The Testament of William Tracy." *Journal of Ecclesiastical History* 44.3 (1993) 415–31.

Cranmer, Thomas. *The Remains of Thomas Cranmer*. Edited by H. Jenkyns. Oxford: Oxford University Press, 1833.

Cuming, G. J. *A History of Anglican Liturgy*. 2nd ed. London: Macmillan, 1982.

Darling, Pamela. *New Wine: The Story of Women's Transforming Leadership and Power in the Episcopal Church*. Boston, MA: Cowley, 1994.

Dickens, A. G. *The English Reformation*. New York: Schocken, 1971.

Dowling, Maria. "Anne Boleyn and Reform." *Journal of Ecclesiastical History* 35.1 (1984) 30–46.

Duffy, Eamon. *The Stripping of the Altars: Traditional Religion in England 1400–1580*. New Haven, CT: Yale University Press, 1992.

Emmanuel College Library. Hugh Latimer to Joan Wilkinson. ECL MS 260, fo. 276v.

——. John Bradford to Joyce Hales. ECL MS 260.

——. Thomas Cranmer to Joan Wilkinson. ECL MS 262.

The First and Second Prayer Books of Edward VI. Everyman's Library. 1910. Reprint, New York: Dutton, 1960.

Foxe, John. *Book of Martyrs*. 1570. https://www.gutenberg.org/files/22400/22400-h/22400-h.htm.

Freeman, Thomas. "Dissenters from a Dissenting Church: The Challenge of the Freewillers, 1550–1558." In *The Beginnings of English Protestantism*, edited by Peter Marshall and Alec Ryrie, 129–56. Cambridge: Cambridge University Press, 2002.

Gloucestershire Record Office. Gloucester Borough Records.

——. Gloucester Diocesan Records.

——. Gloucestershire Wills.

——. St. Michael's Churchwardens Accounts, P154/14 CW 1.

——. Tewkesbury Borough Records B2/1.

Hardwick, C. *A History of the Articles of Religion*. London: George Bell & Sons, 1904.

Hereford and Worcester Record Office. 802 BA 2764.

Hickerson, Megan. "In Control of Conscience: Female Recusancy in Elizabethan England." M.A. thesis, Texas Tech University, 1991.

Hill, H., and J. Watson. "In Christ There Is No Gay or Straight?: Homosexuality and the Episcopal Church." *Anglican and Episcopal History* 75.1 (2006) 37–68. http://www.jstor.org/stable/42612945.

A History of the County of Gloucester, vol. 8. Victoria History of the Counties of England. London: Oxford University Press, 1968.

Bibliography

Hooker, R. *Of the Laws of Ecclesiastical Polity: Preface, Book I, Book VIII*. Edited by Arthur S. McGrade. 5 vols. Cambridge Texts in the History of Political Thought. Cambridge: Cambridge University Press, 1989.

Hooper, John. *Later Writings of John Hooper Together with His Letters and Other Pieces*. Edited by C. Nevinson. Parker Society. Cambridge: Cambridge University Press, 1852.

Hughes, Paul L., and James F. Larkin, eds. *Tudor Royal Proclamations*. 3 vols. New Haven, CT: Yale University Press, 1969.

Hutton, Ronald. "The Local Impact of the Tudor Reformation." In *The English Reformation Revised*, edited by Christopher Haigh, 114–38. Cambridge: Cambridge University Press, 1987.

Kater, John. "Latin-American Anglicanism in the Twentieth Century." In *The Oxford History of Anglicanism, Vol. V, Global Anglicanism, c.1920–2000*, 98–123. 5 vols. London: Oxford University Press, 2019.

Knowles, David. *The Religious Orders of England, vol. III, The Tudor Age*. 3 vols. Cambridge: Cambridge University Press, 1959.

Letters and Papers, Foreign and Domestic of the Reign of Henry VIII. Edited by J. S. Brewer, et al. 21 vols. 1864. Reprint, London: Her Majesty's Stationary Office, 1965.

Litzenberger, Caroline. "Community, Faith and Identity: Women's Will-making in Early Modern England." Presented at the annual Sixteenth Century Studies Conference, Atlanta, GA, 25 October 1997.

———. *The English Reformation and the Laity. Cambridge Studies in Early Modern British History*. Cambridge: Cambridge University Press, 1997.

———. "Evangelical Religious Identity, Gender, and Martyrdom in the Reign of Mary Tudor." Presented at the biennial Reformation Studies Colloquium in Oxford, UK, 5–7 April 2006.

———. "Gender and Religious Identity among the Protestant Divines and their Supporters in the Reign of Mary." Presented at the annual Pacific Coast Conference of British Studies in Riverside, CA, 1–3 April 2005.

———. "Identity Formation and Strategies of Resistance to Elizabethan Religious Policies." Presented at the annual meeting of the North American Conference on British Studies in Boston, MA, 20 November 1999.

———. "Will-making in the Identity Formation of Sixteenth Century English Women." Presented at the annual Sixteenth Century Studies Conference in Toronto, 23 October 1998.

145

MacCulloch, Diarmaid. *The Reformation: A History*. London: Penguin, 2003.

———. *Thomas Cranmer*. New Haven, CT: Yale University Press, 1996.

Marcombe, D. *English Small Town Life: Retford, 1540–1642*. Oxford: Oxford University Press, 1993.

Marshall, Peter. "(Re)defining the English Reformation." *Journal of British Studies* 48.3 (2009) 564–86.

———. *Heretics and Believers: A History of the English* Reformation. New Haven, CT: Yale University Press, 2018.

McGregor, J. F. "Seekers and Ranters." In *Radical Religion in the English Revolution*, edited by J. F. McGregor and B. Reay, 121–39. New York: Oxford University Press, 1984.

Milton, Anthony. *England's Second Reformation: The Battle for the Church of England 1625–1662*. Cambridge: Cambridge University Press, 2021.

Nichols, J. G., ed. *Narratives of the Days of the Reformation; Chiefly from the Manuscripts of John Foxe the Martyrologist; with Two Contemporary Biographies of Archbishop Cranmer*. London: Camden Society, 1859.

Order of Communion. 1548. http://justus.anglican.org/resources/bcp/Communion_1548.htm.

Parkhurst, John. *Letter Book of John Parkhurst*. Edited by Ralph Houlbrooke. Norwich, UK: Norfolk Record Society, 1974/5.

Peters, Kate. *Print Culture and the Early Quakers*. Cambridge Studies in Early Modern British History. Cambridge: Cambridge University Press, 2005.

———. "'Women's Speaking Justified': Women and Discipline in the Early Quaker Movement, 1652–56." In *Studies in Church History* 34 *Gender and Christian Religion* (1998) 205–34. https://doi.org/10.1017/S042420840001367X.

The Prayer Book of Elizabeth, 1559. London: Griffith Farran & Co., 1559. https://www.google.com/books/edition/The_Prayer_book_of_Queen_Elizabeth_1559/cH8RAAAAYAAJ?hl=en&gbpv=1&bsq=ornament.

The Proclamation of the Accession of Queen Lady Jane issued 10 July 1553. https://www.somegreymatter.com/proclamation.html.

Public Records Office. PROB 11/42B.

———. PRO/SP 12/117/12. Bishop Richard Cheyney to the Privy Council, 24 October 1577.

"*Reformatium Legum Ecclessiiasticarum*." In *Tudor Church Reform*, edited by Gerald Bray, 166–69. Church of England Record Society, vol. 6. Woodbridge, UK: Boydell and Brewer, 2000.

"Report of the Joint Commission on Marriage and Divorce." In *The Journal of General Convention of the Protestant Episcopal Church of the United States of America, 1931 / The Archives of Episcopal Church*, App. XI. 480–81. Saint Louis, MO: Frederick, 1932. https://www.episcopalarchives.org/sites/default/files/publications/1931_GC_Journal.pdf.

Scott, Katherine T. "The House of Deputies in the Episcopal Church." In *Shared Governance: The Polity of the Episcopal Church*, 19–28. New York: Church Publishing, 2012.

Statute of the Realm. 8 vols. London: Dawsons, 1963.

Stowe, John. *Three Fifteen-Century Chronicles with Historical Memoranda*. London: Camden Society, 1880. https://www.british-history.ac.uk/camden-record-soc/vol28/pp128-147.

Strype, John. *Annals of the Reformation and Establishment of Religion*. 4 vols. Oxford: Oxford University Press, 1824.

The Testament of Master Wylliam Tracie esquire / expounded both by William Tyndale and Jhon Frith. Antwerp, 1535. STC 24167.

"A True Copy of Bishop Hooper's Visitation Booke, made by Him, A.D. 1551, 1552." Dr. Williams Library. Morice MS 31L.

Tyndale, William. *An Answer to Sir Thomas More's Dialgoue, the Supper of the Lord after the True Meaning of John VI. and I Cor. XI. and Wm. Tracy's Testament Expounded*. Cambridge: Cambridge University Press, 1850.

Verner, L. "Catholic Communities and Kinship Networks of the Elizabethan Midlands." *Perichoresis* 13.1 (2015) 75–97. https://content.sciendo.com/configurable/contentpage/journals$002fperc$002f13$002f1$002farticle-p75.xml.

Visitation Articles and Injunctions. Edited by W. H. Frere and W. P. M. Kennedy. 3 vols. London: Longman, Green, and Co., 1910.

Wabuda, Susan R. "The Provision of Preaching during the Early English Reformation . . . c. 1530–1547." PhD thesis, University of Cambridge, 1991.

Ward, Kevin. *The History of Global Anglicanism*. Cambridge: Cambridge University Press, 2006.

Wark, Keith R. *Elizabethan Recusancy in Cheshire*. Chetham Society, 3rd series, vol. XIX. Manchester: Manchester University Press, 1971.

Westerhoff, John. *A People Called Episcopalians*. The Institute for Pastoral Studies. Rev. ed. Atlanta, GA: St. Luke's Press, 1996.

Woolverton, J. F. "The Chicago-Lambeth Quadrilateral and the Lambeth Conferences." *Historical Magazine of the Protestant Episcopal Church* 53.2 (1984) 95–109. https://www.jstor.org/stable/42974763.

INDEX

Aragon, Catharine of, 25, 61
Armada, 94–95
Aske, Robert, 30
Aylmer, John (Bishop), 96

Baynham, James, 23–24
Bible, 18, 28, 31, 48, 103
   and Erasmus, 8
   and Hooker, 102
   and Lollardy, 10
   and Missionaries, 116, 116n
   and Tyndale (Matthews
      Bible), 21, 68
   and Wycliffe, 10
   Bishop's, 22
   Gospel Paraphrases, 31,
      103
   Gospels, 31, 48, 103
   Great, 21–22
   Injunctions, 31, 43
   King James (Authorized)
      Version, 107
   Scriptures, 4, 5, 7, 9, 18–19,
      32, 42, 97, 101–3, 114,
      122, 124, 128, 138
   Vulgate, 5, 22
Bilney, Thomas, 23–24
Bitner, Merritt, 132
Black Death, 2–3, 5–6, 12,
   15–16, 63, 78, 138
Boleyn, Ann, xvi, 25–26, 33,
   38, 69, 79, 139
Bonner, Edward, 76
Book of Martyrs, 103
Book of Revelation, 110
Bozarth-Campbell, Alla, 132
Broughton, William Grant, 119
Brounsmythe, Thomas, 59
Brown, Thomas, xx–xxi
Burial, xxi, 31
Burning (of heretics), 68

Calvary Episcopal Church,
   Pittsburgh, 115
Calvin, John, 5, 13, 39–40, 60,
   84, 86, 100, 102

Canon Law, 52–53
Canterbury, archbishop of
    Cranmer, Thomas, xvi,
        xix, 25–27, 35, 40, 45,
        52–53, 65, 139
    Grindal, Edmund, 73, 98
    Laud, William, 107–8
    Parker, Mathew, 85, 87
    Whitgift, John, 98, 101
Care, pastoral, 69
Catholic piety, 6
Chaderton, Lawrence, 95
Chambers, Richard, 73
Chantries Act, 44, 49
Charles I, 107, 110
Charles II, 112
Charles V, 25, 75
Chastity, 34
Cheek, Allison, 132
Cheyney, Richard (Bishop), 96,
    96n, 100
Chicago-Lambeth
    Quadrilateral, 122
Choirs, Men and boys, 115
Church Courts, 36, 41, 54, 96
Church of the Advocate,
    Philadelphia, 132
Church, doctrinal, 13, 67, 76
Church, High, 114
Church, Liturgical, 13
Church, Low, 114
Churchwardens Accounts, 41
Clerk, Parish, 48
Clerke, John, 52
Clerke, Walter, 52
Clitheroe, Margaret, 92–93
Conference, Hampton Court,
    106
Conference, Lambeth, 122–23,
    131, 134–36

Conference, Women and
    Ministries, 133
Constable, Henry, 52
Corrigan, Daniel, 132
Council of Basel, 11
Council of Constance, 11
Council of Regency, 37–38
Council of Trent, 76
Council, Fourth Lateran, 9
Council, Second Vatican, 126
Courtenay, Edward, 75
Cox, Richard, 74
Cranmer, Thomas, xvi, 13,
    26–27, 32–33
    and Henry VIII, 25, 35–36
    and Liturgy, 35–36, 47,
        54–55, 126
    and Lutheran writings,
        17, 21
    and Martyrdom, 65, 68,
        71, 72n
    and Religious change, 40–
        41, 44–46, 51, 53–54,
        60, 64, 74, 124–25,
        138–39
    and Spiritual presence, 40,
        55, 100
Cromwell, Oliver, 108, 112
Cromwell, Thomas, 25–27, 30,
    33, 35, 38,
Crowley, Robert, 89–90
Crown, the, xv, 10, 14, 25,
    29–30, 43, 49, 52, 62,
    66–67, 76, 95, 98, 100,
    111–12, 136, 139
Cultural differences, 116

Denominations, Gatherings,
    and Regional Churches
    Anglican Church of
        Aotearoa, New

Index

Zealand, and Polynesia, 120

Anglican church, xiv–xv, 14, 49, 56, 83, 105–6, 116, 119, 121–22, 129, 136–37

Anglican Communion, 106, 113, 115, 122–24, 131, 133–38, 140–41

Anglicanism, xv, 116–17, 120–22

Baptists, 109, 112

Brethren of the Common Life, 7

Calvinism, 82, 102

Calvinists, 72, 74, 83, 86–88, 95, 97, 99, 101, 107, 109

Catholicism, Anglo-, 114, 119–20

Catholicism, Henrician, 35

Catholicism, Marian, xxi, 61–7, 69, 72, 75–76, 78–80, 139

Catholicism, xi, xiv–xvi, 35, 81–3, 87, 90–92, 95, 102, 104, 140

Church Convocation, 86, 87–88, 100

Church of England, xiv, 2, 14, 17, 21, 26, 40, 45, 49, 52, 83, 96, 100, 105–6, 108–9, 112–16, 119, 123, 129, 141

Church of Kenya, 121

Church of Nigeria, 121

Church of Rome, xi, 3, 5–6, 12

Congregationalists, 109

Diggers, 110

Episcopal Church, xv, 13, 117, 121–23, 125–30, 132–34, 136, 140

Hussites, 11, 16

Independents, 109

Lollardy, 9–10, 16

Lutheranism, 26, 67, 120

Methodism, 113

Precisians, 87

Presbyterian, 96, 98, 108

Protestantism, xi, xiv–xvii, xviiin, xix, 1, 10, 12, 15

Puritan, 90, 102

Quakers, 110–11, 112

Radical Religion, 113

Ranters, 110, 112

Recusants, 91–92

Swiss Reform, 39, 40, 44, 50, 52, 56, 84

United Church of Christ, 109

Dauphin, French, 86

Davis, Joan, 57

Device for the Succession, 62–63

DeWitt, Robert, 132

Diocese of Australia, 118–19, 119n

Diocese of Calcutta, 118

Diocese of Gloucester, xviii–xix, 27, 32, 36, 50–51, 54, 57, 63, 67, 77, 79, 84, 89, 92, 96–98, 100

Diocese of New Hampshire, 123, 136

Diocese of New Zealand, 119–20

Diocese of Norwich, 96

Diocese of Polynesia, 120

Diocese of Salisbury, 3, 16

Index

Diocese of Worcester, 26–27, 69

Diversity, xv, xvii, xviiin, 13, 81

Divine authority, 19

Drewett, William, 96–97

Drowry, Thomas, 67–68, 68n

Dudley, John, 38

Dudley, Robert, 86

Dyston, John, 77

Ecclesiastical Polity (of Richard Hooker), 102

Edward VI, xvi, 14, 16, 21, 26–27, 35–37, 39, 49, 52, 74, 89, 138–39

Elite, the, xvi, 3, 6, 21, 29, 31, 35, 61–62, 68, 103, 121

Elizabeth I, xviii, 14, 26, 35, 72, 74, 79, 82, 104, 139

Ellice, John, 52

Endowments, 43–44, 49

Enlightenment, 113

Episcopal Church Women, 130–31

Episcopal Divinity School, 132

Episcopal Joint Commission on the Church and Human Affairs, 134–35

Episcopal United Thank Offering, 130

Erasmus, Desiderius, 7–8, 31

Evangelicalism, 122

Exile, Religious, 62, 66–67

Exiles

English, 72–74, 87, 104

French, 72

Famine, 2–3

Fell, Margaret, 110–12

Fell, Thomas, 110

Fervor, Religious, 113

Fox, George, 110–12

Freewillers, 70

Freke, Edmund (Bishop), 96

Frith, John, 23

Gadding (to sermons), 97

Gardiner, Stephen, 38

Gender, 111, 129, 134–35

Behavior, Gender-coded, 71

Bisexual people, 134, 136

Episcopal Women's Auxiliary of the Board of Missions, 130

Homosexuality, 134–35, 137

Human sexuality, 129, 134–37

Integrity, 134

Lesbians, 134–36

Men, Gay, 134–36

Same-gender/sex unions, 135–36

Transgendered people, 106, 134, 136

Women's roles, 62

Women's-only meeting, 112

General Convention of the Episcopal Church, 117–18, 122, 125–27, 130–31, 133–35

Geographical Places and Regions

Australia, 115, 118–19

Canada, 120, 132

Denmark, 86

France, xvi, 29, 72, 76

German States, 5, 17–18, 73, 117

Global South (of the Anglican Communion), 116, 136

Index

Hong Kong, 131
India, 121
Ireland, 65, 95, 113, 115
Italy, 2, 4, 18, 26
Japan, 121
Mexico, 121–22
Netherlands, xvi, 7, 68, 73
Scotland, 91, 95, 106, 108, 119
Sierra Leone, 121
Spain, 25, 75–76, 86, 94
Switzerland, xi, xvi, 5, 8, 13, 17–18, 62, 73, 87, 137
Global warming, 137
Glover, Mary, 69–70
Great Awakening, 113
Great Depression, 124
Great Schism, 2–3, 6, 15
Grey, Lady Jane, 62–63
Grindal, Edmund, 73, 98
Griswold, Frank, 123, 140
Groote, Gerhard de, 7

Hailes, Joyce, 70
Harris, Barbara, 132
Henry I, 24
Henry II, 24
Henry VIII, 14, 17, 24, 30, 32–33, 35–38,
Hewitt, Emily, 132
Heyward, Carter, 132
Hiatt, Suzanne, 132
Holder, Joan, 77
Holy Roman Emperor, 18, 25
Hooker, Richard, 101
Hooper, Anne, 72
Hooper, John, 27, 36, 63, 89
House of Bishops, 118, 128, 132, 135
House of Commons, 95, 108

House of Deputies, 118, 131
Humanism, Renaissance, 2, 2n, 4, 6–8, 11, 15–16, 18, 138
Humanism, Philology, 4
Humphrey (Humphries), Lawrence, 52, 69
Hus, Jan, 11
Hymns, 18, 115

Indigenous people, 116, 119, 121
First Nation People, 120
Māori, 119–20
Identity formation, xv, xvii, xviiin, 140
Identity, Religious, xv, xvii, 23, 28, 32, 62, 67, 70–71, 140
Influenza, 63, 78–79
Injunctions, Royal, 31, 85
International Consultation on English Texts (ICET), 126

James VI and I, 53, 106

Keble, John, 114
Knox, John, 73–74

Liturgy
Anglican-Roman Catholic International Commission (ARCIC), 126
Apostolic Tradition, The (of Hippolytus), 124
Ash Wednesday, 50, 127
Authorized Services, 127
Baptism, 12, 19, 28, 54, 87–88, 96, 99, 109, 114, 123, 125, 128–29

Liturgy (continued)
   Baptismal Covenant, 128
   Book of Common Prayer,
      17, 40, 60, 100
     and Calvinists, 98, 101
     and *Common Worship* in
       England, 129
     and Cranmer, 26
     in Frankfurt, 73–74
     of 1549, 41, 46–48
     of 1552, 53–56
     of 1559, 84, 88
     New Zealand, 119
     outlawed, 108–9
     Resistance to, 40–49
     United States Episcopal,
      117, 124–25, 127, 138
   Books, Liturgical, 79
   Change, Liturgical, 124,
     137–38
   Collect for Purity, 54
   Common Worship, 129
   Communion Bread, 46, 56,
     84, 99
   Communion Host, 6,
     45–46, 51
   Communion in Both
     Kinds, 34, 40, 44
   Communion Wafer, 34, 85
   Confession, 28, 34, 36,
     40–41, 127
   Confirmation, 128
   Creed, 31, 123, 125
   Creeping to the Cross, 50
   Daily Offices, 47–48, 127
   *Directory for the Public
     Worship of God*, 108–9
   *Draft Proposed Prayer
     Book*, 127
   Easter Sepulcher, 50, 52
   Elevation of the host, 6

Episcopal Standing
   Liturgical Commission,
   125, 127
Eucharist, 9, 12, 14, 20, 28,
   40–41, 55, 100, 114,
   123, 125, 127, 133
Evening Prayer, 47, 84
Gloria, 54, 125
Holy Communion, see
   Eucharist
Invocation of the Holy
   Spirit, 41, 54, 117
Lectionary, 128
Litany, 37, 41–42
Lord's Prayer, 31
Martyr, Justin, writings
   of, 124
Mass, 6, 16–17, 20, 32,
   41, 45–46, 48, 52, 59,
   64–65, 77, 83, 93, 126
Matins, see Morning
   Prayer
Morning Prayer, 47, 84
Order of Communion,
   44, 46
Order of Geneva, 74
Ornaments Rubric, 96
Palm Sunday, 50, 125, 127
Prayer Book (see *Book of
   Common Prayer*)
Prayer Book Studies, 125
Prayer for the Sevenfold
   Gifts of the Spirit, 128
Prayer for the Whole State
   of Christ's Church, 54
Prayer of Consecration, 46,
   51, 117, 125
Primers, 46
Renewal, liturgical, 124
Sacraments, 8, 10, 12,
   19–20, 123, 125–26

Index

Sarum rite, 16

Ten Commandments, 31, 42, 54, 103

The Peace, 54, 125

Trial Use, 126

Visitation Articles and Injunctions, 40, 42, 84

Words of Administration, 54–55, 63

Worship practices (see also Worship), xix, 5–6

Worshipping Community, 72

Laity, xiv, xviii–xix, 3, 6, 17, 23, 29, 31–34, 40, 42, 48, 50, 52, 62, 65, 69, 72, 77, 83, 95, 106, 108, 117–18, 136

Latimer, Hugh, 26–29, 32–33, 36, 65, 68–69, 69n

Latimer, William, 27

Laud, William, 107–8

Learning, New, 2n, 4–5

Leicester, Earl of, 86

Lex Credendi, 12

Lex orandi, 12

Lichtenberger, Arthur, 131

Living, William, 51–52

Lord Protector, 38, 49, 108

Luther, Martin, xi, 5, 7–8, 12, 17–22, 26, 35, 39–40, 55

Marprelate Tracts, 98

Marriage
　Annulment, Henry VIII, 25
　Divorce, Episcopal General Convention, 134
　Divorce, Henry VIII, 25
　Elizabeth I, 85–86, 90
　Episcopal General Convention, 134–35

Henry VIII, 25, 35
　Mary I, 75–76, 79

Martyrdom, 27, 66, 69

Mary I, xvi, 61–65, 71, 84, 139

Mary, Bloody (see Mary I)

Medieval church, 2, 5, 106, 115

Merchants xvi, xviii, 17, 20, 72, 139

Merchants, Wool, 6, 32

Missionaries
　Church Missionary Society, 116, 119, 121, 126
　Colonialism, 137
　East African Revival Movement, 121
　Society for the Propagation of the Gospel, 121
　Universities' Mission to Central Africa, 121

Monasteries, 27, 29–30, 35, 47

More, Thomas, 8

Morefield, Marie, 132

Movement, Cambridge, 105, 114

Movement, Oxford, 105, 114

Myton, John, 59

Naylor, James, 111

Newman, John Henry, 114

Nobles, Northern, 91

Norfolk, Duke of, 49

Northumberland, Duke of, 38, 49

Nowell, Alexander, 87

Orders, ordained
　Deaconesses, 131
　Deacons, 87, 131, 133
　Presiding Bishop, 118, 123, 131, 134, 140
　Priesting of women, 131, 134

Oi, Florence Li Tim, 131
Out of charity, 94

Places and regions
    Antwerp, 74
    Avignon, 2, 3
    Bohemia, 11
    Bolton, 31
    Bristol, xx, 111
    Cambridge, xvi, 7–8, 17,
        20–21, 89, 95, 105, 107,
        114–15
    Chipping Camden, 6
    Christchurch in Devon, 31
    Cirencester, xviii–xix, 6, 32
    Cornwall, 49
    Cotswolds, 32
    Coventry, 70
    East Anglia, 32–33, 86, 89
    Emden, 72
    Fairford, 7
    Forest of Dean, 24, 27–29,
        32, 36, 38
    Frankfurt, 69, 72–74
    Geneva, 72, 74, 84, 102
    Georgia, 118
    Gloucester, xiii, xviii–xix,
        54, 79, 84, 96–97
    Hadleigh, xviii–xix, 21,
        51–52, 59, 65
    Hasfield, 92
    Lavenham, 6
    Lincolnshire, 30
    London, 24, 27, 33, 50, 63,
        66, 68, 87, 89, 97
    Malmesbury, 31
    Mendlesham, 23
    Minneapolis, 127, 133
    Norfolk, 31, 49, 63

Oxford, xvi, 9, 11, 17,
    20–1, 68, 89, 105, 107,
    114, 138
Pershore, 31
Philadelphia, 117, 132
Provinces, Northern
    (of Anglican
    Communion), 136
Queen's College,
    Cambridge, 8
Shrewsbury, xviii–xix,
    59, 90
Smithfield, 24, 68
Strasbourg, 72–73
Tewkesbury, xviii–xix, 30
Trinity College,
    Cambridge, 114
Tudenham, 51–52
Westbury-on-Severn, 23
Wymondham, 31
Yorkshire, 30, 110
Zurich, 72, 84
Papacy, 1–2, 25, 27, 65, 139
Papist, church, 91
Parker, Mathew, 21, 85, 87
Parr, Katherine, 35
Patronage, 26
Pauncefoot, John, 92
Peter's Pence, 9
Philip the Fair, 2
Phillip II, 86
Pickard, Jeanette, 132
Pilgrimage, 29
Pious practices, 1, 4, 15, 29, 32,
    37, 45, 76–77
Plague (see Black Death)
Pole, Reginald, 65, 76
Policy, Official Religious, xv,
    xvii, 24–25, 44, 51–52,
    58, 71, 85, 87, 91, 95,
    103, 109, 140

Poor, the, 10, 20, 40
Pope John XXIII, 126
Preachers, xvi, 27–29, 32–33, 70, 111
Preachers, Licensed, 32, 45, 111
Predestination, see the elect
Priests, Catholic, 92–93
Priests, women, 132–34
Privy Council, 33, 35, 37, 75, 91, 96n
Proclamation, Royal (of Mary I), 64–65
Protectorate, 108, 112
Protestant wind, 95
Pusey, Edward Bouvarie, 114

Quakers
    Divine spark, 110–11
    Inner Light of Christ, 110–11
    Swarthmore Hall, 110
    Worship, Quaker, 111

Racism, 106, 137
Religion, New, xi, xvi, 12, 45, 49, 58–59, 66, 82, 140
Religion, Old, 5–7, 32, 90
Religious change, xiv–xvi, xix, xxi, 7, 11, 14–15, 17, 26, 38, 41, 43–44, 49, 57, 59, 65, 83, 95, 139–40, 141
Religious confusion, 105, 107–13
Renewal, Liturgical, 106, 124–29, 138
Republican, form of Government, 108–9
Resistance, religious, 48–49, 71, 84, 90–95
    Book smuggling, 26

    Break with the Church of Rome, 32, 53, 139
    Civil War, English, 108
    in Cornwall, 49
    In Norfolk, 49
    Papal Challenges, 138
    Papal Chaos, 2
    Papal Schism, 16
    Pilgrimage of Grace, 30
    Priest holes, 93
    Prison, Newgate, 97
    Prophesyings, 98
    Ridolphi Plot, 91
    Sermons, Disrupting, 111
    Treason, 26, 90, 93, 108
Ridley, Nicholas, 21, 50, 65, 68
Robinson, Gene, 123, 135
Rogers, John, 21, 68
Rosary, 51, 94

Sandys, Edwin, 88
Scheiss, Betsy Bone, 132
Schori, Katherine Jefferts, 134
Selwyn, George Augustus, 119
Sermons
    Book of Homilies, 45, 101
    Letter, 69–70
    licensed, 111
    Lively (extemporaneous), 97, 101
Seymour, Edward, 38
Shepherd, William, 23
Silkwomen, xvi, xvin, 27
Somerset, Duke of, 49
Spanish Match, 76
Spiritual whiplash, 14
St. Giles-without-Cripplegate, London, 89
St. John's College, Cambridge, 89
St. Mary's, Bury St. Edmunds, 32
St. Mary's, Hadleigh, 92

St. Michael's, Gloucester, xiii, xviii–xix, 54, 79, 84
St. Michael's, York, 7
St. Nicholas, Gloucester, 96
St. Paul's Cathedral, London, 86, 88
St. Wendreda's, March, Cambs., 32
Statutes
    Act against Revilers, 44
    Act of Six Articles, 34
Stuart, Mary (Mary, Queen of Scots), 90–91, 106
Superstition, 29, 42
Supreme Head, 25
Swanson, Karina Welles, 132

Theology, 3, 8, 11–13, 18, 28, 32, 37, 39, 51, 70, 102, 110, 114
    Baptism, Believer's, 87
    Belief, 12–13, 20, 22, 28, 55, 59, 100, 102, 110–11, 114
    Books, 17, 20–21, 27, 31, 33, 38, 46, 69, 74, 101, 139
    Church Doctors/Father, 4, 5
    Commemoration, 20, 55–56, 100
    Devotio moderna, 7, 12
    Elect, the, 9, 19, 112
    Heresy, 24, 67–68, 76
    Holy Spirit, 41, 54, 117–18
    Holy Water, 28–29
    Idolatry, 42, 52
    Idols, 20, 40, 44
    Images, 20–21, 31, 40–44, 50, 52, 56, 64, 76, 79
    Levitical Code, 24
    Millenarianism, 110

Prayers for the Dead, 32, 43–44, 47, 114
Purgatory, 43
Real presence, 28, 55–56, 100, 114
Sola fide, 19
Sola scriptura, 19
Spiritual Presence, 55, 100
Thirty-nine Articles, 87, 100
Transubstantiation, 9–11, 20, 34, 55, 87, 100, 114
Taylor, Rowland, xix, 21, 51, 65
Tracy, William, xx, 22
Tudor, Mary (see Mary I)
Tyndale, William, 21–23, 33

Vernacular, 18–19
Vestments, 41, 52–54, 64, 79, 82, 84, 88–89, 90, 95, 99, 102, 115
    Alb, 41, 84
    Chasuble, 41, 84
    Cope, 41, 84
    Geneva Gown, 84, 89
    Square cap, 88
    Surplice, 41, 53, 84, 90, 96
    Vestarian Controversy, 95
Virgin Queen, 86

Warcup, Ann, 69–72
Warcup, Cuthbert, 69, 72
Washington National Cathedral, 115
Welles, Edward, 132
Wentworth, Peter, 95
Westerhoff, John, 13
Whitgift, John, 98, 101
Wilkinson, Joan, 27, 69, 70, 71
Wills, xviii–xxi, 23, 36–37, 41, 52, 57–59, 77–78, 140
    Will preamble, xix–xx, 23

Will Scribes, xix–xx, 36
Will Soul bequest, xix
Will Testators, xix–xxi,
    22–23, 57–59, 77, 132
Wittig, Nancy Hatch, 132
Wolsey, Cardinal, 24
Women, Elite, 68
Worship, 14, 18
    and Church papists, 92–94,
        99–100
    and images, 20, 41
    and Recusants, 92, 99–100
    and Scripture, 48, 102–3
    and vestments, 84, 89
    Calvinist, 108
    Change in, xix, 5, 8, 13,
        17, 40–41, 45, 48–51,
        53–54, 56, 60, 64, 74,
        88, 100, 113–15, 124,
        126–29, 139–40
    Disruption of, 44, 101
    Early church, 12
    Emotion in worship, 113
    Enthusiasm in worship, 113
    in Frankfort, 72–74
    Lutheran, xvi, 25
    Prayer Book (with or
        without), 97–98, 101,
        108, 109
    Protestant under Mary I, 66
    Traditional (Catholic), 6,
        34, 36, 51, 64, 76, 78

Ranters, 112
Worship space, xviii, 31, 41–
        43, 49–50, 53, 56, 64,
        73, 99, 103
    Altar, xiii, 6, 14, 41, 46, 50,
        53, 56, 64, 78, 84, 107
    Beauty of holiness, 107
    Candlesticks, 42
    Chancel, 50, 54, 64, 84, 103
    Chantry Chapels, 6, 32,
        43–44
    Choir Pews, xiii, 54
    Church interiors, 33, 76
    Church Plate, 52
    Communion Table, 41,
        53–54, 56, 103
    Nave, 6, 30, 41, 50, 54, 56,
        103
    Pulpit, 43, 76, 90, 94, 99,
        101, 103, 111
    Rood loft, 64, 78–79
    Sanctus bell, 6
    Tapers, 42, 52
    Trestle Table, 53
    Wall Paintings, 56
    Wax, 42
    Whitewash, 42, 53
Writings, Lutheran, xvi, 17, 21
Wycliffe, John, 9–10

Zwingli, Ullrich, xi, 5, 8, 12,
        17–20, 22, 39, 40, 55